Out of Control

...and lovin' every minute of it!

Gail Knox

May the Word of
God bless you
in every way!

April Knox

This Book is Dedicated to:

my partner in ministry,
Susan E. Woodward, co-founder,
Word Among Us Ministries,
who encouraged the writing of this book

my husband,
David R. Knox, who single-handedly kept our radio
program
"The Word Among Us" on the air
so I would have time to write this book

my Heavenly Father,
who supplied the inspiration, stamina, time, and all
creative skills
for the writing of this book

and my son,
B. Michael Knox, who led me into a saving
relationship with Jesus Christ
*so I would be **available** to write this book.*

Contents

Introduction

A merica is facing spiritual crisis. The enemy sits on the very brink of victory, and believers are poised for the great fall.

A hundred years or so ago, sanctuaries on Sunday mornings resonated with refrains of "I Surrender All," "Have Thine Own Way Lord," "Trust and Obey" and the like. Believers incorporated the language of surrender into every corner of their lives: We are not our own; we were bought at a price. Our bodies are the temple of the Lord, cleanliness is next to godliness, early to bed, early to rise... the list goes on and on.

But somewhere along the way, surrender became an ugly nine-letter word. Un-American even. Its usage metamorphosed into a synonym for defeat. Our language turned instead to winning at all cost, becoming the master of our fate and the god of our universe. We talked in terms of fighting to the finish, rising to the top, becoming all that we could be, getting all that we deserve, grabbing the gusto. We were Americans and Americans don't surrender.

The church followed suit. Hymns like "I Surrender All" were removed from at least one mainstream church's hymnal. Words like bondservant and slave were smoothed over for more palatable euphemisms that didn't force the issue of total and irrevocable commitment. Rather than boasting of bondage to God, we focused on finding the purpose of our lives and worked at "doing" things for God by doing things for others. Not surprisingly, the focus of our lives began to shift from God to Self.

It's time to stop and re-examine the relationship of the true believer to his God. It's time to call a spade a spade and acknowledge our total and complete dependence on the One who created and continues to give us life. It's time to get back to basics and realize that success is not measured by the externals of wealth and power, but by the things inside that God sees in us everyday. It's time to yield control of our lives to the One who controls all things. We are not the master of our own lives. We belong to Him.

When it comes to defining the Christian walk, there is no room for ambiguity. The Bible tells us exactly how we are to live our lives and what value we're to place on the "things" we've gathered around us. While God's way may appear un-American to some, it is the one true and narrow path to real happiness. In this book , we aim to awaken in each of us the courage to walk in His way rather than to continue in our own. Only one resource is necessary for such a study and that resource is the Word of God, the Bible, the scriptures, whatever you prefer to call it.

A word of warning to the serious reader. Turning control of your life over to God the Almighty may be a little discom-bobulating at first—especially if you are a control-freak like me. I invite you, therefore, to begin this journey as a mere act of obedience and to trust God solely to flesh out the details according to His own good and perfect will for your life. Then as surrender becomes the discipline of your life, you will find that dependence on Him brings a freedom like none you have ever experienced before.

Part I

Understanding the Call to Surrender

CHAPTER ONE

What Is the "S" Word?

O ne of the greatest gifts God has given me is what I call the "simple life." Don't get me wrong—that's not what I always dreamed of having. I grew up poor and, like just about every other citizen of this great planet, I aspired to becoming rich. God had other plans for me.

It's not whether we are rich or poor that matters—it's who's in control of our lives that defines who we are. I spent forty-four years at the helm of my own life and I cannot say with any degree of honesty that I did a very good job of it. I made some money, I impressed a few people, I bettered myself socially and economically, and all this met a number of my personal goals. Still, I had the nagging feeling that I lacked something really important.

Long about the age when our parents would have been thinking about slowing down, I was confronted by the God who wanted my life for His own purpose. He'd tried to reach me many times before, but this time He finally got my attention. As a result of that first reciprocated encounter with Him, I made the conscious decision to relinquish control of my life to a Heavenly Father. For a control-freak like myself, that was quite the amazing step of faith.

Before going any deeper into the meat of this book, I urge you to take a minute and reflect on your own life. I mean seriously consider who's at the helm. Who is the one who makes the decisions in your life? We're talking about the big decisions here—like where you're going to work and live, whether you're going to have a family or not, to what degree you're going to serve Christ and in what capacity. But we're also talking about the little decisions as well: "Where will I eat today, who will I eat with, how will I spend my free time tonight?" In other words, we're talking about every aspect of our lives.

When I finally decided for myself to let the decision-maker be Christ Jesus instead of Self, the transfer of power from me to Him didn't take place over-night. I wish I could say that it did, but I can't. It is a process—a lengthy one that's still going on today. The same is probably true for much of the Christian population. Turning control of our lives over to Jesus isn't easy because it doesn't feel natural. It feels more like giving up or quitting, and *that*'s against our basic up-bringing. The more natural thing is to fight to maintain control for ourselves. And that's exactly what we do.

Looking at the "S" Word in Scripture

When we talk about turning control of our lives over to Jesus, I'm going to refer to it with what I call the "S" word—surrender—that yielding of power over what we do, say, think and feel to the One who created us.

No form of the actual word "surrender" appears in either the King James Version or the New American Standard Bible. However, the New International Version uses it in one form or another at least eighteen times. All but two of these occur in the Old Testament.

Each time we read the word "surrender" in the New International Version (NIV), its meaning is easily discerned and completely non-debatable: the yielding possession-of or power-over to another outside ourselves. In all sixteen of the Old Testament references, the context is that of a nation's militarily giving itself up to another, said nation having been conquered by the opposing army. This meaning of surrender carries the heavy implication of defeat and failure. In the two New Testament references, the meaning is similar but refers to the condition of an individual rather than that of a military power. In the first of these references (Luke 23:25), the word is used when Pilate gives Jesus over to the people for them to do as they choose.

> **He [Pilate] released the man who had been thrown into prison for insurrection and murder, the one they asked for, and surrendered Jesus to their will.** [Luke 23:25, NIV]

In this use of the word, we hear a little of the military surrender coming through, yet without any idea of real defeat attached to it. In the other New Testament reference (1 Corinthians 13:3), "surrender" refers to the giving up of one's own body to a dreadful fate. Nothing military, nothing involving defeat—just the *voluntary* yielding of power over oneself to someone or something outside oneself.

> **If I give all I possess to the poor and surrender my body to the flames, but have not love, I gain nothing.** [1 Corinthians 13:3, NIV]

The differences are subtle, but noteworthy. It's this latter meaning of the word that we are addressing in this book—the voluntary yielding possession-of or power-over our own lives to the one true God who loves us more than our feeble minds can possibly grasp. We can learn even more about this word by looking at the pictures God paints for us in the Bible. The word surrender does not appear in any of these passages, but its implication is clear. Let's begin with Jesus in the garden of Gethsemane, early on the morning of the very day on which He suffered death on the cross.

> **Jesus went out as usual to the Mount of Olives, and his disciples followed him. On reaching the place, he said to them, "Pray that you will not fall into temptation." He withdrew about a stone's throw beyond them, knelt down and prayed, "Father, if you are willing, take this cup from me; yet not my will, but yours be done." An angel from heaven appeared to him and strengthened him. And being in anguish, he prayed more earnestly, and his sweat was like drops of blood falling to the ground.**
> [Luke 22:39-44, NIV]

As you read this passage, what sense do you get of Jesus' mental and emotional being at that time? The references to being in anguish, praying more earnestly, and sweating something that resembles "drops of blood" jump out and alert us to the fact that Jesus was facing something He definitely didn't want to do. "Father," He says, "... take this cup from me." Make no bones about it, Jesus didn't want the cup. He's asking God to take it away and all that it represents, leaving us hard-pressed to imagine anything so horrific that Jesus would cry out in such anguish.

A common explanation from some very learned Bible scholars points to the up-coming death Jesus would endure on the cross. Jesus knows that in less than twenty-four hours

16

He will be nailed to a cross, and then the cross will be lifted up and dropped into a hole in the ground. The jolt of that drop will cause the weight of His body to rip against the spikes driven through His hands and feet. Then as He hangs on the crossbar through the heat of the day, exposure and dehydration take their toll on His internal organs, birds of prey peck at His flesh and the muscles of His chest constrict to snuff out the last of His breath. Eventually. Could such a torturous demise be the "cup" to which Jesus refers, and from which He desires relief from God? I don't know about you but it just doesn't seem likely to me that the Messiah who never sinned in any way would agonize so intensely over the physical condition of the body.

Scripture is our best commentary on scripture, so let's turn again to the Bible for clarification.

> **Then the angel carried me away in the Spirit into a desert. There I saw a woman sitting on a scarlet beast that was covered with blasphemous names and had seven heads and ten horns. The woman was dressed in purple and scarlet, and was glittering with gold, precious stones and pearls. She held a golden cup in her hand, filled with abominable things and the filth of her adulteries.** [Revelation 17:3-4, NIV]

We need to consider the meaning of the "cup" in this passage from the book of Revelation. The woman dressed in purple and scarlet holds a golden cup in her hand. The cup is a picture of the sum-total of all the sins of her life—the "abominable things and the filth of her adulteries," scripture reads.

> **God made him who had no sin to be sin for us, so that in him we might become the**

17

righteousness of God. [2 Corinthians 5:21,
NIV]

In this passage from 2 Corinthians, God tells us that Jesus
will be sin for us. He doesn't say that Jesus will *commit* sin
(Jesus is perfect and remains perfect; without sin), but that
Jesus will *be* sin on our behalf. If you find this a little difficult
to understand, don't dismay. This is not an easy teaching.
The theological term for what's going on here is "imputa-
tion"—that reckoning (attributing or crediting) of something
to an individual's account. It's not earned or deserved, but
rather it's attributed to an individual *as if* he or she had actually accomplished it on his own. The same principal is at
work as when God considers us righteous not because of our
own good but because of the righteousness of Christ. In this
case, God will consider Jesus "sin" not because of Jesus'
sinful acts but because of the sinfulness of all mankind. One
concept is merely the flip-flop of the other.

So! Jesus became sin for you and me. In Romans 6:23
we read that "...the wages of sin is death," and so we know
that at the exact moment Jesus becomes sin, He suffers
spiritual death and is separated from God. An unfathomable
thought! That God the Son would be separated from God the
Father... even if only for a brief nanosecond! Even though
they are three (Father, Son and Holy Spirit), they are one
(Deuteronomy 6:4). And "One" cannot be separated without
dire consequences.

If we use the Revelation 17 picture printed out above of
the woman dressed in scarlet and purple with the golden cup
in her hand and relate this picture to the cup in Jesus' prayer,
we see that both are dealing with the sins of the world. Like
the cup the woman in scarlet holds, the cup Jesus is to drink
might also be filled with abominations and the filth of sin—
not His own, but the sins of the world. Viewed in this way,
we have little difficulty in understanding the anguish Jesus

would experience as He anticipated the certainty of the cross that would separate Him from the Father. The evidence is heard in His cry from the cross: "My God, My God, why have you forsaken me?" [Mark 15:34]

Doing the Will of God

If you do not remember, look back at Luke 22:39-44 and determine what Jesus says *after* His plea to have the cup taken from him. "Yet not my will," He says, "but yours be done." As much as He didn't want to experience that separation from the Father, He wanted *more* to be smack-dab in the middle of God's will. *This* is our model for the surrendered life. Jesus lived it out so that you and I would know exactly what God expects of us. He painted the picture so we can have no doubt as to how we're supposed to live. The second chapter of Paul's letter to the saints in the church at Philippi puts it this way:

> **Your attitude should be the same as that of Christ Jesus: Who, being in very nature God, did not consider equality with God something to be grasped, but made himself nothing, taking the very nature of a servant, being made in human likeness. And being found in appearance as a man, he humbled himself and became obedient to death — even death on a cross! [Philippians 2:5-8, NIV]**

Examine that first line carefully. "Your attitude should be the same as that of Christ Jesus..." Your *attitude,* it says—that's what's inside you, your thoughts, yours feelings, your perceptions. So the Bible is telling us that what's inside us should be the same as what's inside Jesus. That's a tall order. But an order it is. The Greek verb used in this first sentence is in the present tense, imperative mood, active voice. This indicates that God is giving us a command to do something which involves continuous or repeated action from here on out. What is He wanting us to do? Clearly, it's to have the same thoughts and feelings inside us that Jesus does. Layering this, then, over Jesus' prayer in the Garden of Gethsemane we see that no matter how desperately we want NOT to do something, we should want *more* to be smack-dab in the middle of God's will. In other words, our first priority is Him and not Self. Our desires, dreams and purposes are all surrendered to His. Totally and completely.

We'll return to this subject in later chapters as we explore in detail what the surrendered life looks like. For now, we need to grasp the basic principal that for us Jesus is the model—the standard that we are to follow. Look again at the Philippians 2 passage above, this time focusing on the second half of the first sentence: "Who, being in very nature God, did not consider equality with God something to be grasped..." Let's stop right here and gather together what we already know from reading just this far. Even though Jesus *is* God, we see He does not demand or cling to His rights as God. Is He equal to God? Absolutely! According to John 10:30, He and the Father are one. If anything is "one," it's the same, identical; equal. So Jesus and the Father *and* the Holy Spirit are all equal. Yet, how does Jesus choose to consider Himself in Philippians 2? Let's read on at verse 7. "...but made Himself nothing, taking the very nature of a servant..."

We explore the subject of servanthood thoroughly in Part 2 of this book, "What the Fully Surrendered Life Looks Like." What I want you to see here is what Jesus *chooses* to do. Instead of demanding His rights as God, He does what? He "makes Himself nothing," the NIV tells us. The original Greek here is *kenoo* which means to make empty. In other words, the text in Philippians 2 is telling us that Jesus *empties* Himself of all that is rightfully His. Are we starting to get the idea of what the surrendered life is all about?

So many of us genuinely desire serving our Lord in all that we do, yet hang on to the American ideal of being in complete control of our own destiny. It ain't happening, folks! We cannot give our lives to Jesus and keep them for ourselves at the same time. We must put aside our idealistic notions and look at what Jesus did in giving up control of His life. He surrendered fully, He emptied Himself, He made Himself nothing. We've already established that God commands believers to have the same attitude as Jesus, so what else could this mean than we have to surrender our lives as well?

The True Believer Must Surrender to His Lord

Here's the substance of what we've been saying so far: any believer who sincerely desires to serve God must learn to surrender his or her life in the manner Jesus laid out for us. Will it be easy? Of course not. That's the purpose of this book—helping the committed believer to blossom into the believer whose life is fully surrendered to God.

CHAPTER TWO

Fearing God for Who He Is

Fundamental to our surrendering to God is our having a right relationship with Him.

Among the first things we learn in our Christian walk is the fact that our God is a God of love. We like that. Everyone wants to be loved, so we naturally latch on to this unconditional love concept with the tenacity of a bulldog. "God loves me no matter what," I can remember using almost as a mantra when I first became a Christian. "I don't deserve His love, but He loves me anyway." "Even though I make bunches of mistakes, He keeps right on loving me." What a concept! Who doesn't want that for his own life?

For me personally, this new knowledge brought a relief that was more than I could wrap my mind around. Growing up, I never really knew the love of an earthly father. My dad was a good man but he was away a lot of the time on business. Even when he was home, he never showed much affection. When I was ten, my mother was diagnosed with terminal cancer; she died when I was twenty and was sick much of the time in between. You can imagine how I didn't get much love from her either because of a natural preoccupation with survival against the odds of cancer. When I learned that God loved me so much He gave up His Son for me, I was stunned—overwhelmed. From that point on, all I wanted to hear was how much I was loved. Why would I ever want to study anything but the love of God? In fact, as I tackled my earliest studies of scripture, I rejected all the teachings about the other side of God's character—His wrath. "That's the God of the Old Testament," I would tell myself. "I'm not under the Old Testament" and I'd go on with my digging into the New Testament writings, not at all concerned about the fact that I was ignoring huge chunks of the Bible.

People who talk *only* about God's love don't have the whole picture.

God *is* love—no doubt about it. The Bible is clear about that. But in order to see God solely as a God of love, one has to ignore a great deal of the written word. A lot of well-meaning Christians, when confronted with scripture that shows the expiration of God's patience (in other words, His wrath), will counter with the argument: "How could a loving God do that?" They blame the devil for every bad thing that comes their way. We need to understand that God is the God of love *and* He is the God of wrath. Hard as that is for mere mortals to understand, it's absolute truth.

Furthermore, we cannot ignore teachings in the Old Testament that give pictures of God's wrath in action. In Malachi 3:6, we are told that God does not change. So if wrath is a part of His character in the Old Testament, it's a part of His character in the New. We just have to get used to that fact and quit trying to rewrite the Bible to fit our own misconceptions.

God Mandates Fear

We will deal more with the topic of God's wrath in Chapters 4 and 5 that address the sovereignty of God and the free will of man, but it's important to note here that God's wrath leads us to a very important conclusion concerning our relationship with Him. There's a movement afoot in recent history that encourages us to regard God as our friend. There's definitely a right way and a wrong way to go about this (See Chapter 12, "Life as The Friend of God"); however, God is not, never has been—never *will* be—our pal, our buddy, our equal. He is God, and as such, He is to be feared. That's the topic of this chapter—the Biblical mandate to fear God.

Let's look first at Jesus' teaching in the tenth chapter of Matthew:

> [16]I am sending you out like sheep among wolves. Therefore be as shrewd as snakes and as innocent as doves.
>
> [17]Be on your guard against men; they will hand you over to the local councils and flog you in their synagogues. [18]On my account you will be brought before governors and kings as witnesses to them and to the Gentiles. [19]But when they arrest you, do not worry about what to say or how to say it. At that time you will be given what to say, [20]for it will not be you speaking, but the Spirit of your Father speaking through you.
>
> [21]Brother will betray brother to death, and a father his child; children will rebel against their parents and have them put to death. [22]All men will hate you because of me, but he who stands firm to the end will be saved. [23]When you are persecuted in one place, flee to another. I tell you the truth,

you will not finish going through the cities of Israel before the Son of Man comes.

²⁴A student is not above his teacher, nor a servant above his master. ²⁵It is enough for the student to be like his teacher, and the servant like his master. If the head of the house has been called Beelzebub, how much more the members of his household!

²⁶So do not be afraid of them. There is nothing concealed that will not be disclosed, or hidden that will not be made known. ²⁷What I tell you in the dark, speak in the daylight; what is whispered in your ear, proclaim from the roofs. ²⁸Do not be afraid of those who kill the body but cannot kill the soul. Rather, be afraid of the One who can destroy both soul and body in hell. [Matthew 10:16-28, NIV]

The crux of Jesus' teaching here is found in verse 28. In the preceding verses, He addresses the Twelve as He sends them out to spread His teachings throughout the land. Much like our own earthly fathers do as they launch us into adulthood, He gives instruction and explains to His beloved disciples the opposition they can expect along the way. He knows they will encounter dangerous situations and He exhorts them not to "be afraid of those who kill the body but cannot kill the soul." As unpleasant as the verbal and physical abuses are, He says they are nothing compared to what God is capable of dishing out. Jesus states it this way: "Rather, be afraid of the One who can destroy both soul and body in hell." Who could Jesus be referring to here if not the Father Himself? No one has the authority to send body and soul to hell except the One who created man and is sovereign over all the universe. Bottom line then, Jesus is telling us we should fear *whom*? You got it—we are to fear God! Why? Because of what God can do to us.

The Luke account of this makes the point even stronger.

But I will show you whom you should fear: Fear him who, after the killing of the body, has power to throw you into hell. Yes, I tell you, fear him. [Luke 12: 5 NIV]

Let's be sure we understand the full impact of what we're reading here. Those who emphasize God's love and ignore His wrath cannot help but take issue with the statement that we are to fear God. Quite obviously, there's nothing to fear in someone who expresses *only* love. They might explain that when God uses the word "fear" He really means "reverential awe." Well of *course* we are to revere God; of *course* we are to be in awe of Him. And there are many times in scripture when the reference is to reverential awe, but what's the context of Matthew 10? Does it appear to be dealing with reverential awe, or is it more about our being afraid of something that can cause us great harm and suffering?

We can look back at Matthew 10:16-25 and pick out some of the things Jesus says are going to happen to the Twelve: being flogged, being brought before kings, betrayed, hated. Do any of these sound like something the Twelve should revere or be in awe of? Of course not. When Jesus tells them not to fear the men who are able to do these things to them, clearly it has nothing to do with reverence and awe; it has everything to do with being afraid of bodily harm. Common, everyday, run-of-the-mill fear. Now, if that's what the verb means in the first half of the sentence, when Jesus uses the same verb in the second half we would expect the same meaning. In other

27

words, the Twelve should be more "afraid of" God than they are of the beatings and abuses of men. Why? Because God is the One who destroys body and soul in hell, and eternity in hell is something everyone should fear.

Scripture has much to say about the benefits that are enjoyed by those who fear God. Promises abound—promises of prosperity and the receipt of God's goodness, wisdom and knowledge, protection. These are not small things. Clearly God desires that we fear Him if He rewards us for doing so. [Psalm 25:12-13, 31:19, 33:8, 33:18; Proverbs 9:10, 1:7, NIV]

There is No Fear in Love

Okay then, back to our text in Matthew 10:28. This and the other references tell us in no uncertain terms that we should be afraid of God. On the other hand, there are other references that seem to be telling us something entirely different. For example:

> **There is no fear in love. But perfect love drives out fear, because fear has to do with punishment. The one who fears is not made perfect in love.** [1 John 4:18, NIV]

At first glance, this verse appears to be in conflict with the Matthew 10 passage. We know that's impossible, however, because 2 Timothy 3:16 tells us that all scripture is God-breathed. If all scripture comes out of the mouth of God, then all scripture is truth. The reader's challenge becomes one of finding the single interpretation that allows both truths to coexist without manipulation.

Let's examine our observations from these two passages. The Greek word translated "be afraid of" in Matthew 10:28

[NIV] is the verb form of the noun translated "fear" in 1 John 4:18. So in essence, we're dealing with the same word in each passage. Yet, the imperative in Matthew 10 directs us to fear God and 1 John 4:18 tells us that if we have perfect love we will have no fear. How do we reconcile these two thoughts?

We've already established the fact that the Matthew 10 passage is not talking about our relationship with men, but about our relationship with God. It's all about our having a healthy respect for the power God has to determine our eternal state. To what, then, is the "fear" in 1 John 4:18 referring? For an answer to that, we need to consider the context in which verse 18 resides:

> **¹²No one has ever seen God; but if we love one another, God lives in us and his love is made complete in us.**
>
> **¹³We know that we live in him and he in us, because he has given us of his Spirit. ¹⁴And we have seen and testify that the Father has sent his Son to be the Savior of the world. ¹⁵If anyone acknowledges that Jesus is the Son of God, God lives in him and he in God. ¹⁶And so we know and rely on the love God has for us.**
>
> **God is love. Whoever lives in love lives in God, and God in him. ¹⁷In this way, love is made complete among us so that we will have confidence on the day of judgment, because in this world we are like him. ¹⁸There is no fear in love. But perfect love drives out fear, because fear has to do with**

**punishment. The one who fears is not made
perfect in love.** [1 John 4:12-18, NIV]

When we read verse 12 we see that God's love is made
complete (also translated "perfect") in us as a result of His
living in us. What kind of person is this describing? What
do we know is true about the man who has God abiding in
him? This is the picture of the true believer, is it not? God in
him. And verse 15 makes an even stronger point: "If anyone
acknowledges that Jesus is the Son of God, God lives in him
and he in God." God lives in the one who acknowledges
Jesus as the Son of God; in other words, God lives in the true
believer and His love is complete (perfect) in him. This is the
context in which we approach verses 17 and 18: God's love
is total, complete, perfect within the true believer.

Verse 17 tells us that believers have this perfect love
so that they will not fear the judgment. And, of course, we
know the believer has no need to fear the judgment because
he has already been judged and declared righteous. So, in
the Matthew text, we are to fear God because He has the
power to judge and send us to hell; and this is true. But in the
1 John text, we see that believers have no reason to fear the
judgment itself because we are already saved. In essence, the
passages are talking about different sides of the same coin.
So even though they may sound as if they're in a conflict, we
see that both are in fact true.

Intrinsic in all that we're saying about fearing God is
the premise that we are able to trust God—a subject we will
address in the next chapter.

Before we move on to the subject of Trust, however, we
need to take a quick look at the last sentence in 1 John 4:18:
"The one who fears is not made perfect in love." Can God
make it any clearer? He's giving us the reciprocal here; He's
telling us that not only is the saved person without fear of
judgment but if a person is afraid of the judgment, he is not

saved. (He has not been "made perfect in love.") This is one of the many reasons I find study of the Bible so fascinating. God gives us a truth; then He turns right around and states that same truth in another way, just to make sure that we don't miss the point. It's as if He were saying, "Make no mistake about it. This is the way it is." I like that. It makes the Bible so understandable.

Fear Makes Surrender Possible

In the first chapter of this book, we learned that if a believer sincerely desires to serve his God, he or she must learn to surrender his life in the same manner that Jesus did. Now we see that surrender is contingent upon our possessing a healthy fear of God—a fear not so much of what He does, but of what He is *capable* of doing. Quite obviously, then, in order to have a relationship with God in the midst of the fear He demands of us, there must be a huge amount of trust involved.

And that is the topic of our next chapter.

31

CHAPTER THREE

Trusting Our Lord in What He Does

No discussion of "fear" is complete without looking at
its flip side.

In the last chapter, we established Jesus' command that
we are to fear God. The New International Version actually says we are to be afraid of Him. It is natural to ask,
then, what kind of relationship can we possibly have with
someone we're afraid of? Is it possible to feel close to
someone we fear?

At one end of the spectrum, there's a fear totally void
of any trust at all; at the other end, a fear totally wrapped—
ENVELOPED—in trust. Think about the fear you would feel in
the presence of a maniacal tyrant who's capable of maiming,
torturing, killing you on a whim. On the other hand, there's
the fear you experience when facing life-threatening surgery
at the hands of a skilled surgeon who has your best inter-
ests at heart and a perfect record in the OR. Two different
fears—one with, and one without trust. Most life situations
fall somewhere in between.

The Need for Trust

We can look to our everyday social interactions for insight. In the parent-child relationship, for example, the child fears the parent's authority to discipline and have physical supremacy over her. The child has learned that if she doesn't do as told, she will incur the wrath of the parent. Yet the child continues to love the parent in spite of this fear. Why? Because she knows that she is loved by that parent and she trusts him to do what is right. Trust. In order for the child to submit voluntarily to the authority of a parent, she must first trust. Otherwise, the human spirit rebels.

When it comes to our relationship with God, the same reasoning applies. If we do not trust God, the fear we have of His power to annihilate us will preempt any relationship we might otherwise have. On the other hand, if we *do* trust God, the fear He demands no longer serves as a deterrent to our enjoying a close and special relationship with Him. It should, in fact, have the opposite effect—bringing the believer closer to his God.

First Biblical Use of Trust

The first mention in scripture of the word "trust" is found in Genesis 22, when God appears to Abraham and commands him to take his son—his "only son" Isaac—to Mount Moriah and to offer him as a burnt offering there. We'll pick up the story with Abraham's response to God's order.

> **[3]Early the next morning Abraham got up and saddled his donkey. He took with him two of his servants and his son Isaac. When he had cut enough wood for the burnt offering, he set out for the place**

**God had told him about. ⁴On the third day
Abraham looked up and saw the place in
the distance. ⁵He said to his servants, "Stay
here with the donkey while I and the boy
go over there. We will worship and then
we will come back to you."** [Genesis 22:3-5,
NIV]

Already we learn something about Abraham. He is
obedient. "Early the next morning" after God speaks to
him, Abraham packs for the journey and immediately sets
out according to God's instructions. At this point, he doesn't
even know the exact location of the destination... just that
it's one of the mountains in the region of Moriah. So rather
than picking out his own way, Abraham is forced to follow
God's lead every step of the way.

We're beginning to get a picture of what "trust" is all
about.

What does Abraham say to his servants after arriving
in the region? What does he tell them about what he and
the boy are going to do? It's quite clear when he says *"we*
will worship and then *we* will come back to you" (emphasis
mine), he has no expectation of returning without a very
much alive son. Not that he doubts that God wants the sacrifice to occur; but rather, he's trusting God to do something
spectacular in typical "God-style" that will allow Isaac to
return with him.

**⁶Abraham took the wood for the burnt
offering and placed it on his son Isaac, and
he himself carried the fire and the knife.
As the two of them went on together, ⁷Isaac
spoke up and said to his father Abraham,
"Father?"**

> **"Yes, my son?" Abraham replied. "The fire and wood are here," Isaac said, "but where is the lamb for the burnt offering?"**
>
> **⁸Abraham answered, "God himself will provide the lamb for the burnt offering, my son." And the two of them went on together.** [Genesis 22:6-8, NIV]

What is the first manifestation of trust we see in these verses? Abraham tells his son that he's expecting God to provide the lamb for the sacrifice. Now, we know that Abraham knows that God wants him to sacrifice his son Isaac. Is he lying to his son when he tells him that God will provide a lamb for the sacrifice? We've already read the clue that tells us otherwise. Back in verse 5, he told his servants that he would return *with the boy*. So when he tells Isaac in verse 8 that "God himself will provide," he may not know exactly *how* but he certainly trusts God to do something. What did he believe? The Faith Chapter in Hebrews has something to say about that.

> **By faith Abraham, when God tested him, offered Isaac as a sacrifice. He who had received the promises was about to sacrifice his one and only son, even though God had said to him, "It is through Isaac that your offspring will be reckoned." Abraham reasoned that God could raise the dead, and figuratively speaking, he did receive Isaac back from death.** [Hebrews 11:17-19, NIV]

Abraham believed in the resurrection of the dead *and* he trusted God. So he reasoned that if God had promised a great nation through his son Isaac, then even if God ordered Isaac killed, quite obviously God would resurrect the boy after the slaughter. Now *that's* trust!

> **⁹When they reached the place God had told him about, Abraham built an altar there and arranged the wood on it. He bound his son Isaac and laid him on the altar, on top of the wood. ¹⁰Then he reached out his hand and took the knife to slay his son. ¹¹But the angel of the Lord called out to him from heaven, "Abraham! Abraham!"**
>
> **"Here I am," he replied.**
>
> **¹²"Do not lay a hand on the boy," he said. "Do not do anything to him. Now I know that you fear God, because you have not withheld from me your son, your only son."** [Genesis 22:9-12]

What's the word God gives Abraham here? Did you catch it? "Now I know that you [*What?*] fear God [*Why?*] because you have not withheld from me your son, your only son." This is what it's all about. Abraham's actions demonstrate his trust in God, and God refers to that trust with the phrase, "Now I know you *fear* God" (emphasis mine.) The connection between fearing God and trusting Him—the two are inseparable if we're to have any kind of relationship with God.

What happens to Abraham when he couples his fear of God with absolute trust? Let's read on at verse 13.

> **¹³Abraham looked up and there in a thicket he saw a ram caught by its horns. He went**

over and took the ram and sacrificed it as
a burnt offering instead of his son. ¹⁴So
Abraham called that place The Lord Will
Provide. And to this day it is said, "On the
mountain of the Lord it will be provided."

¹⁵The angel of the Lord called to Abraham
from heaven a second time ¹⁶and said, "I
swear by myself, declares the Lord, that
because you have done this and have
not withheld your son, your only son,
¹⁷I will surely bless you and make your
descendants as numerous as the stars in
the sky and as the sand on the seashore.
Your descendants will take possession of
the cities of their enemies, ¹⁸and through
your offspring all nations on earth will be
blessed, because you have obeyed me."

¹⁹Then Abraham returned to his servants,
and they set off together for Beersheba.
And Abraham stayed in Beersheba.
[Genesis 22:13-19, NIV]

Clearly in Abraham's case, blessings follow obedience.
We see that same principle illustrated throughout his life—
God commands, Abraham obeys, God blesses. It's a simple
formula that's just as applicable to our lives today. Granted,
the blessings may not always follow as close as we like.
Granted, there are times when we must exercise that part of
our "fruit of the spirit" called patience, but they *do* follow.
God's promises are simply facts that have not yet occurred.
The Bible is clear on this: we must trust God.

The Virgin Mary Trusted God

Perhaps the most shining of all "trust" examples in scripture concerns the young girl to whom the angel Gabriel appears and advises that she will give birth to the Son of God. The gospel of Luke gives us the most detailed description we have of that event.

> **[26]In the sixth month, God sent the angel Gabriel to Nazareth, a town in Galilee, [27]to a virgin pledged to be married to a man named Joseph, a descendant of David. The virgin's name was Mary. [28]The angel went to her and said, "Greetings, you who are highly favored! The Lord is with you."**
>
> **[29]Mary was greatly troubled at his words and wondered what kind of greeting this might be. [30]But the angel said to her, "Do not be afraid, Mary, you have found favor with God. [31]You will be with child and give birth to a son, and you are to give him the name Jesus [32]He will be great and will be called the Son of the Most High. The Lord God will give him the throne of his father David, [33]and he will reign over the house of Jacob forever; his kingdom will never end." [Luke 1:26-33, NIV]**

Can you imagine the shock of hearing such words? Especially if you're a girl of only thirteen or fourteen years old, unmarried and a virgin. Skeptics try to twist our understanding of this encounter so as to wring all significance out of the virgin birth. Belief in the virgin birth is critical to the value of the incarnation itself, and that makes it critical to

all Christianity. For obvious reasons, these critics want to
convince us that the term "virgin" in verse 27 means *only*
that she was a young girl of marriageable age. Indeed, there
are other places in scripture where the word appears to have
such a meaning. We will see, however, as we read on in this
passage in Luke that God makes it quite clear that Mary was
all this and *more*.

> ³⁴"How will this be," Mary asked the angel,
> "since I am a virgin?" [There's that word
> again.]
>
> ³⁵The angel answered, "The Holy Spirit
> will come upon you, and the power of the
> Most High will overshadow you. So the
> holy one to be born will be called the Son
> of God. ³⁶Even Elizabeth your relative is
> going to have a child in her old age, and
> she who was said to be barren is in her
> sixth month. ³⁷For nothing is impossible
> with God." [Luke 1:34-37]

Mary's response to angel Gabriel's proclamation is one
of bewilderment. She does not dispute what the angel says,
nor express doubt or disbelief concerning it; rather, she
simply states her wonder at such an incredible thought: she,
of all people; she, a virgin—the mother of Messiah!
   Let's take a closer look at the word that's translated
"virgin" in verse 34. The original Greek here is *not* the same
word as the one translated "virgin" in verse 27. Pick up
different translations of the Bible and you'll see that trans-
lators have used more than one word to express the same
thought. The New International Version, the New American
Standard Bible, the New Living Translation and The Living
Bible all read "...I am a virgin." The King James Version,

however, gives us more of a clue as to the literal words used in the original text. "...I do not know a man." You probably already see what's going on here. We're dealing with a euphemism, much as was popular in our own language during the early years of the 20th century and before. To "know" someone intimately was the polite phrase of the day to express having sexual intercourse. When Mary responds to Gabriel's news that she will bear a child, it is clear that she is saying that she has never had sexual intercourse with a man—how could she possibly have a baby? It would have been physically impossible.

How does Gabriel respond to Mary's bewilderment? He assures her that nothing is impossible with God. Now, the birth of a baby to a young girl of marriageable age (as some claim the word "virgin" to mean) is certainly possible; but birth of a baby to a woman who has never had sexual intercourse is impossible. Obviously, the angel knew exactly what Mary meant when she called herself a "virgin."

And regardless of how overwhelming all this must have seemed to Mary, she accepts what she hears.

> **38"I am the Lord's servant," Mary answered. "May it be to me as you have said." Then the angel left her.** [Luke 1:38, NIV]

We cannot help but make the connection between Mary's words here and Jesus' prayer at Gethsemane when He said: "Yet not my will, but yours be done." [Luke 22:42, NIV] Both were facing traumatic issues; both trusted God fully for the outcome. They wanted it to be God's call and not their own. That's trust. And that's what God wants from us.

Mary's Song

In our last chapter we talked about how we are commanded to fear God and how this fear must be coupled with absolute trust if we are to have the relationship with God He calls us to. We easily see the trust in Mary's reaction to God's call on her life, but does she have the fear to go along with it? She appears to respond so coolly to the startling news of motherhood that we might be tempted to conclude she has no fear. Let's pick up the scriptures a little further down in the first chapter of Luke and listen to the song Mary sings in praise of her Lord.

> **[46]And Mary said: "My soul glorifies the Lord [47]and my spirit rejoices in God my Savior, [48]for he has been mindful of the humble state of his servant.**
>
> **From now on all generations will call me blessed, [49]for the Mighty One has done great things for me—holy is his name. [50]His mercy extends to those who fear him, from generation to generation. [51]He has performed mighty deeds with his arm; he has scattered those who are proud in their inmost thoughts. [52]He has brought down rulers from their thrones but has lifted up the humble. [53]He has filled the hungry with good things but has sent the rich away empty. [54]He has helped his servant Israel, remembering to be merciful [55]to Abraham and his descendants forever, even as he said to our fathers." [Luke 1:46-55, NIV]**

Verse 50 of the song makes it clear that Mary believes God extends mercy to all who fear Him. Implicit in her trust in God to handle this unwed-mother thing is her dependence on his mercy. Based on Mary's own words concerning the connection she perceives between mercy and the "fear of God," it is evident that Mary herself also fears God.

Fear of God and trust. Without the one, the other is empty. Mary, mother of Jesus, shows with her life the inseparable connection between the two.

Shadrach, Meshach and Abednego

Another favorite Bible illustration concerning trust involves three fellows who are being held captive in a foreign land. Their lot as part of a conquered nation would not have been so bad if only they obeyed the wishes of the conquering ruler, but unfortunately for them some of the king's edicts violated their religious tenets. Listen to one of these edicts that came out of the king's office.

> [4]Then the herald loudly proclaimed, "This is what you are commanded to do, O peoples, nations and men of every language: [5]As soon as you hear the sound of the horn, flute, zither, lyre, harp, pipes and all kinds of music, you must fall down and worship the image of gold that King Nebuchadnezzar has set up. [6]Whoever does not fall down and worship will immediately be thrown into a blazing furnace."
>
> [7]Therefore, as soon as they heard the sound of the horn, flute, zither, lyre, harp and all kinds of music, all the peoples, nations

**and men of every language fell down and
worshiped the image of gold that King
Nebuchadnezzar had set up.** [Daniel 3:4-7,
NIV]

This is the story of Daniel's three friends: Shadrach,
Meshach and Abednego during their captivity in Babylon at
the hands of King Nebuchadnezzar. All four of these guys
were considered the crème de la crème of the Jewish aristoc-
racy and as such enjoyed special favor at the hand of the king.
However, even they were expected to fall down and worship
the golden image. In the passage above, we read about the
decree's being made. The passage below focuses on the
response of Shadrach, Meshach Abednego to that decree.

**[8]At this time some astrologers came
forward and denounced the Jews. [9]They
said to King Nebuchadnezzar, "O king, live
forever: [10]You have issued a decree, O king,
that everyone who hears the sound of the
horn, flute, zither, lyre, harp, pipes and all
kinds of music must fall down and worship
the image of gold, [11]and that whoever does
not fall down and worship will be thrown
into a blazing furnace [12]But there are some
Jews whom you have set over the affairs
of the province of Babylon—Shadrach,
Meshach and Abednego—who pay no
attention to you, O king. They neither
serve your gods nor worship the image of
gold you have set up."**

**[13]Furious with rage, Nebuchadnezzar
summoned Shadrach, Meshach and
Abednego. So these men were brought**

before the king, [14]and Nebuchadnezzar said to them, "Is it true, Shadrach, Meshach and Abednego, that you do not serve my gods or worship the image of gold I have set up? [15]Now when you hear the sound of the horn, flute, zither, lyre, harp, pipes and all kinds of music, if you are ready to fall down and worship the image I made, very good. But if you do not worship it, you will be thrown immediately into a blazing furnace. Then what god will be able to rescue you from my hand?" [Daniel 3:8-15, NIV]

Clearly, Shadrach, Meshach and Abednego love their Lord and will have no other god before Him, regardless of the suffering their loyalty might bring them. Apparently, such devotion is outside King Nebuchadnezzar's realm of understanding and he gives them yet one more opportunity to bow before *his* sovereign authority. Perhaps he thought the first decree, since it was issued to all the people, might have seemed impersonal and easy for them to ignore; this one was up close and personal—the King himself was talking to them face-to-face. Surely these intelligent young men would see the wisdom in yielding to the dominion of their king and comply with his wishes.

[16]Shadrach, Meshach and Abednego replied to the king, "O Nebuchadnezzar, we do not need to defend ourselves before you in this matter. [17]If we are thrown into the blazing furnace, the God we serve is able to save us from it, and he will rescue us from your hand, O king. [18]But even if he does not, we want you to know, O king, that we will not serve your gods or worship

the image of gold you have set up." [Daniel 3:16-18, NIV]

Our God will save us! But even if He does not... Facing a gruesome and horrible death, these three men in the prime of their lives, chose to trust God, even at the risk of death. They knew beyond a shadow of a doubt that their God was able to save them; they trusted him to do so. But—and that's the key word here—but *even if* their God chose not to rescue them, their faith wouldn't dissolve. They would continue to trust Him for whatever outcome He chose for them.

What was the result God sent their way? If we read on at verse 19, we see that the King was furious and ordered the furnace heated seven times its normal temperature before throwing the three men into it. Immediately, a fourth man appears in the fire—one Nebuchadnezzar said looked like a son of the gods. Nebuchadnezzar approaches and orders Shadrach, Meshach and Abednego to come out of the fiery furnace. The threesome emerges unscathed!

They trusted God with the results and God did not disappoint His subjects.

Shadrach, Meshach and Abednego feared God enough not to compromise their allegiance to Him by falling down before idols—even when failure to do so would cost them their lives. They trusted Him enough to surrender their future into His hands—absolutely.

Trust Makes Surrender Possible

Fear and absolute trust go hand in hand to bring us into a right relationship with God. Fear without trust builds barriers against a healthy relationship. Since we cannot surrender to God without first attaining that right relationship, we must couple trust with the fear Jesus commands of us.

CHAPTER FOUR

Acknowledging the Sovereignty of God

By nature, we human beings are selective. Especially when it comes to surrendering control of our lives to anyone or anything outside ourselves.

Up to this point, we've talked about the unnaturalness of surrender and how we must first fear God and then trust Him before we will ever be able to turn our lives over to Him. Now in this chapter, we add a third dimension that impacts our ability to turn loose and give in to God. It works like this: (1) We fear God; (2) we trust Him; and then, (3) we acknowledge Him as sovereign over *all* things. This means that we believe nothing has greater power than He, that when push comes to shove, God always has the last word, that nothing happens without His knowledge and consent. I use the word "always" here and "always" means what? Always. Not sometimes—but all the time. Many pay lip service to such a belief; living it out in one's life is a different matter—especially when sometimes it *appears* bad things are happening to good people.

This is a huge topic. We won't even try to answer every question that comes up—our aim is merely to explore the

Biblical premise that God is in control, even when it seems the whole world is running amuck. God's in control in the midst of chaos, He's in control when bad things happen, He's in control no matter the outcome or the circumstances. Bottom line: He's always in control (there's that word "always" again).

Let's turn to scripture to learn how this premise plays out.

Joseph Understood the Sovereignty of God

One of the sweetest examples of the extent of God's control over man and events (i.e., His sovereignty) is given to us in the concluding chapters of Joseph's life. You know the story. The boy Joseph angers his brothers with his boasting about grandiose dreams and flaunting the gifts his father had given him. His jealous brothers sell him into captivity and deceive father Jacob into believing that Joseph has been devoured by an animal. Ultimately Joseph ends up in the Egyptian household of Potiphar, an official of Pharaoh and captain of the guard. There, Joseph prospers until jealousy again drives him out... this time into prison on the false charge of molesting the master's wife. In prison, Joseph prospers until his ability to interpret dreams earns him an audience before the Pharaoh, and ultimately a position as second in command over all the land.

While Joseph is overseeing the accumulation of food during the seven years of plenty and its distribution during the subsequent seven years of famine, he is visited in Egypt by his brothers from Canaan. Their reunion leads to the family's moving to Egypt where they continue to prosper until the death of father Jacob. At their father's death, the brothers become concerned that their evil deeds against Joseph might come back to haunt them.

> [15]When Joseph's brothers saw that their
> father was dead, they said, "What if Joseph
> holds a grudge against us and pays us back
> for all the wrongs we did to him?" [16]So they
> sent word to Joseph, saying, "Your father
> left these instructions before he died:
> [17]'This is what you are to say to Joseph: I
> ask you to forgive your brothers the sins
> and the wrongs they committed in treating
> you so badly.' Now please forgive the sins
> of the servants of the God of your father."
> When their message came to him, Joseph
> wept. [Genesis 50: 15-17, NIV]

Many of us may be thinking that, given the circumstances,
we would have reacted the same way. Guilty consciences
have a way of rearing their ugly heads long after we're
forgiven and making us doubt the genuineness of the forgiveness that should have brought relief. While it may have been
natural for Joseph's brothers to react in this fashion, the question remains: Was it reasonable? Fear of retribution would
have been valid *only* if Joseph still blamed them for what had
happened. "Does he?" For an answer to that, we need to go
back a few chapters to Genesis Chapter 45 to see what he said
when confronting them with who he was.

> [4]Then Joseph said to his brothers, "Come
> close to me." When they had done so, he
> said, "I am your brother Joseph, the one
> you sold into Egypt! [5]And now, do not be
> distressed and do not be angry with your-
> selves for selling me here, because it was to
> save lives that God sent me ahead of you.
> [6]For two years now there has been famine
> in the land, and for the next five years there

**will not be plowing and reaping. ⁷But God
sent me ahead of you to preserve for you a
remnant on earth and to save your lives by
a great deliverance.**

**⁸"So then, it was not you who sent me here,
but God. He made me father to Pharaoh,
lord of his entire household and ruler of all
Egypt.** [Genesis 45:4-8, NIV]

He says it twice: (1) "God sent me ahead... to preserve
for you a remnant on earth and to save your lives by a great
deliverance"; and (2) "...it was not you who sent me here,
but God..." How could the brothers have missed what he
was saying? God was in control when *they* did what they
did. He had a purpose for their doing it. And had they not
done it, God would have surely seen to it that someone did!
The plan was to save Israel from extinction by starvation; to
do so, God had to get them to Egypt where there would be
food. He chose to do it through the brothers' mistreatment
of Joseph.

It's the sovereignty of God we're hearing here in
Genesis 45. And it is clear that Joseph understands what
they are dealing with. Because of his acknowledgement of
God's sovereignty, we know he holds no grudge against his
brothers. Yet, the brothers slide right over the point and we
see that their concern is not rational.

Let's continue with our Genesis 50 text. Because they fear
retribution from Joseph, the brothers have come to Joseph
with a message from their father begging him to forgive the
brothers. Sounds like Jacob also underestimated Joseph's
affection for his brothers and his willingness to dismiss all
that they had done to him.

¹⁸**His brothers then came and threw them-selves down before him. "We are your slaves," they said.**

¹⁹**But Joseph said to them, "Don't be afraid. Am I in the place of God? ²⁰You intended to harm me, but God intended it for good to accomplish what is now being done, the saving of many lives. ²¹So then, don't be afraid. I will provide for you and your children." And he reassured them and spoke kindly to them.** [Genesis 50:18-21, NIV]

You intended to harm me, Joseph declares to his brothers, but God intended it for good! God's the One in control. He affects the end result. He has authority over men and events. We could go on and on, but the teaching is clear: God is sovereign. God is sovereign. God is sovereign!

The Bible Claims God's Sovereignty

Before we look at other stories that illustrate God's sover-eignty at work, let's look at just a few of the men and events over which God claims sovereignty. Key phrases are printed in italics for your ease in reading. I encourage you to take your time with this; don't try to rush through the reading in order to get it behind you as quickly as possible. You will be blessed if you just sit back, reflect, and enjoy these praises to God.

> **How awesome is the Lord Most High, the great King over *all the earth*!** [Psalm 47:2, NIV]

Let them know that you, whose name is
the Lord—
that you alone are the Most High over *all
the earth.* [Psalm 83:18, NIV]

You will be driven away from people and
will live with the wild animals; you will
eat grass like cattle. Seven times will pass
by for you until you acknowledge that the
Most High is sovereign over *the kingdoms
of men* and gives them to anyone *he wishes.*
[Daniel 4:32, NIV]

[12]For the sins of their mouths, for the words
of their lips,
let them be caught in their pride. For the
curses and lies they utter,
[13]consume them in wrath, consume them
till they are no more.
Then it will be known to the ends of the
earth that *God rules over Jacob.* [Psalm
59:12-13, NIV]

I know that you can do all things;
no plan of yours can be thwarted. [Job 42:2,
NIV]

I cry out to God Most High,
to *God, who fulfills his purpose for me.*
[Psalm 57:2, NIV]

The Lord Almighty has sworn, "Surely,
as I have planned, so it will be, and as I
have purposed, so it will stand..." For the
Lord Almighty has purposed, and who can

> **thwart him? His hand is stretched out, and who can turn it back?** [Isaiah 14:24 & 27, NIV]

> **⁹Remember the former things, those of long ago; I am God, and there is no other; I am God, and there is none like me. ¹⁰I make known the end from the beginning, from ancient times, what is still to come. I say: My purpose will stand, and I will do all that I please.** [Isaiah 46:9-10, NIV]

These passages remind us that God is sovereign over all creation. Nothing exists that has more power than He. Nothing exists that can escape His control. His work, His plan will unfold no matter the obstacles others bring against it.

Job Shows Us God's Sovereignty

Then as we look at the life of Job, we see another illustration of God's sovereignty in action. The Bible tells us that Job was a God-fearing man, blameless, upright, and turning away from evil. One day when the angels are gathering before God in heaven, Satan is among them and the Lord addresses Satan concerning His servant Job.

> **⁸Then the Lord said to Satan, "Have you considered my servant Job? There is no one on earth like him; he is blameless and upright, a man who fears God and shuns evil."** [Job 1:8, NIV]

Did you catch the significance of what God says here? He's the One *initiating* the question. He's the One asking Satan if he's ever thought about Job— not the other way around. Satan merely responds by fielding the proposition God tosses his way.

> ⁹**"Does Job fear God for nothing?" Satan replied. ¹⁰"Have you not put a hedge around him and his household and everything he has? You have blessed the work of his hands, so that his flocks and herds are spread throughout the land. ¹¹But stretch out your hand and strike everything he has, and he will surely curse you to your face."**
>
> ¹²**The Lord said to Satan, "Very well, then, everything he has is in your hands, but on the man himself do not lay a finger."**
>
> **Then Satan went out from the presence of the Lord.** [Job 1:9-12, NIV]

So what does Satan do with the ball God tosses him? He turns it into a test for Job—a test he's convinced that Job will fail. Once Job loses the goodness of God's protection and the material wealth God has provided, Satan believes Job's faith will evaporate. In other words, Satan believes that Job loves the Lord only for what God can, and has done for him. Let's read on and see what actually happens after God *allows* Satan to test Job as he pleases.

> ¹³**One day when Job's sons and daughters were feasting and drinking wine at the oldest brother's house ¹⁴a messenger came**

to Job and said, "The oxen were plowing and the donkeys were grazing nearby, ¹⁵and the Sabeans attacked and carried them off. They put the servants to the sword, and I am the only one who has escaped to tell you!" [Job 1:13-15, NIV]

This was just the beginning of Satan's attack. Almost immediately, another messenger arrives on the scene and announces the death of Job's sheep and his shepherds. Then yet another comes and tells him about a raid and the killing of his camels and all the servants tending them. Finally, a fourth messenger comes with the news that his sons and daughters have all been killed by a freak wind that struck their house and brought it crashing down upon them.

First, everything Job owns; then, everything he loves! With all that bad news, how would you react if you were Job? For many believers, their faith remains strong as long as things are going relatively well. When things blow up, however, they feel as though God has deserted them. And the grumbling begins.

Let's examine Job's reaction.

²⁰At this, Job got up and tore his robe and shaved his head. Then he fell to the ground in worship ²¹and said: "Naked I came from my mother's womb, and naked I will depart. The Lord gave and the Lord has taken away; may the name of the Lord be praised."

²²In all this, Job did not sin by charging God with wrong-doing. [Job 1:20-22, NIV]

Job didn't waiver, he didn't sin, he didn't blame God. This is the epitome of someone who fears God, who trusts God, and who acknowledges God's right to do whatever God pleases! Hard to imagine such devotion, but Job knew it wasn't about him; it was all about God. Obviously, Satan's belief in the vulnerability of Job's faith was unfounded.

The principal lesson for us in Job's ordeal is found in its teaching about how real faith holds up under pressure. That's the same lesson we explored in Chapter 3 with the story of Shadrach, Meshach and Abednego. It's about trusting God no matter the outcome.

There's another lesson in the Job story, though, that we don't want to overlook. We touched on it briefly in our discussion of verse 8 above. In that verse, we see that God *initiated* the challenge to Satan to consider His servant Job. Look down farther a few verses, and in verse 12 we see that God gives Satan permission to torment Job. That's a pretty strong implication that Satan could not have touched Job without God's consent. In addition, God is setting the limits to which Satan is allowed to go. Again, Satan cannot do anything that God does not allow him to do. What are we seeing? The sovereignty of God—no power, not even Satan, can stand against Him.

Jesus Speaks of God's Sovereignty

Satan's inability to act without God's permission is further illustrated in Jesus' comments to Peter in Luke 22:31-32.

> [31]"Simon, Simon [Peter], Satan has asked to sift you as wheat. [32]But I have prayed for you, Simon, that your faith may not fail. And when you have turned back,

strengthen your brothers." [Luke 22:31-32, NIV]

Obviously, Satan had in mind some sort of attack on Peter. Before we look at the point I want to pull out of this, let's not miss the fact that Jesus does not pray that Peter will be spared the temptation, but rather that Peter's faith will be sufficient to carry him through the temptation. That's an important concept for us to remember; it can help in getting us through a rough spot of temptation ourselves.

The big thing I want us to see here, however, is the fact that Jesus says Satan has *asked* to sift Peter as wheat. In other words, before Satan could do what he wanted, he had to clear it with God! Hear the sovereignty of God in this? No power, not even Satan, has any authority other than what God chooses to give to him. That means quite simply that nothing and no one can get to us unless first filtered through the fingers of God's love!

We can see this precept clearly demonstrated in Jesus' mockery of a trial and the execution that followed. Peter talks about it in the speech he gives after the events of Pentecost. While speaking to the crowd of Jews that had gathered, he explains that the phenomenal happenings they had just witnessed with the tongues of fire and the speaking in different languages were not the results of early morning drinking. Instead, he relates what happened to the prophecy Joel had given hundreds of years before. And that in turn leads to a testimony about Jesus. Listen to Peter's explanation of the crucifixion.

[22]"Men of Israel, listen to this: Jesus of Nazareth was a man accredited by God to you by miracles, wonders and signs, which God did among you through him, as you yourselves know. [23]This man was

**handed over to you by God's set purpose
and foreknowledge; and you, with the
help of wicked men, put him to death by
nailing him to the cross. ²⁴But God raised
him from the dead, freeing him from the
agony of death, because it was impossible
for death to keep its hold on him."** [Acts
2:22-24, NIV]

How was Jesus handed over to the Jews for crucifixion?
Whose hand was involved? The answer is stated for us in
verse 23: It was "God's set purpose and foreknowledge." In
other words, it was God's prearranged plan! Nothing was
out of control; nothing running amuck. God knew exactly
what He was doing and His plan was unfolding exactly as
He intended.

Jesus' Death Demonstrates God's Sovereignty

This is not an easy teaching. So God, in His mercy, repeats
it over and over in scripture so that we can be sure that we're
not misunderstanding. One such example is given a few
pages later. Peter and John have just healed the man who
has been crippled since birth and are preaching the name of
Jesus and resurrection from the dead. They are arrested and
spend the night in jail. Upon their release, Peter and John go
back to their own people and report all that has transpired.

**²⁴When they [the people] heard this, they
raised their voices together in prayer to
God. "Sovereign Lord," they said, "you
made the heaven and the earth and the
sea, and everything in them. ²⁵You spoke**

by the Holy Spirit through the mouth of
your servant, our father David:

" 'Why do the nations rage and the peoples
plot in vain?
[26]The kings of the earth take their stand
and the rulers gather together against the
Lord and against his Anointed One.'

[27]"Indeed Herod and Pontius Pilate met
together with the Gentiles and the people of
Israel in this city to conspire against your
holy servant Jesus, whom you anointed.
[28]They did what your power and will had
decided beforehand should happen." [Acts
4:24-28, NIV]

First of all, how do the people address their heavenly
Father in this prayer? They call Him, "Sovereign Lord."
Why? Because that's who He is—sovereign Lord, the One
in control, the One whose power is subject to none other.
See how impossible it is to read more than a few words in
scripture without being reminded of the sovereignty of God?
That's what I love so much about reading the Bible. God
pounds His teachings in again and again so as to be sure that
I don't go off half-cocked in my interpretation!

Specifically, what do the people acknowledge before
God regarding the heinous acts that led to the crucifixion of
Jesus? Verses 27 and 28 give us the answer. The people know
that Herod and Pontius Pilate met together for the purpose of
conspiring against Jesus. The significant truth they confess
is the fact that Herod and Pilate could only do what God's
"power and will had decided beforehand should happen."
Nothing that took place leading up to and including the
crucifixion happened without God's foreknowledge *and* His

permission. Every act by a human being occurred according to God's eternal will and plan. This is why in the garden of Gethsemane, Jesus was asking *God* to remove the cup from Him. Clearly, He knew God was in control and not man.

Jesus made this truth even plainer to us when, at His trial, He responded to Pilate's arrogant (and very foolish) claim to having authority over Jesus.

> [10]**"You won't talk to me?" Pilate demanded. "Don't you realize that I have the power to release you or to crucify you?"**
>
> [11]**Then Jesus said, "You would have no power over me at all unless it were given to you from above..."** [John 19:10-11a, NLT]

There you have it in a nutshell. Throughout scripture we become increasingly aware that our Lord is in control of all things. He is sovereign over all existence.

Sovereignty Makes Surrender Possible

We began the chapter with an acknowledgment that we mortals have difficulty in relinquishing control to anyone or anything outside ourselves. If we're going to follow Jesus' example and surrender ourselves totally and completely to the Father as He did, it's natural we would want assurance that there is no other power greater than His—that once we surrender all that we are to the Father, there is no one or no thing that can overpower Him so as to make us surrender again to someone else.

God is good. In His word, He makes it abundantly clear that His power is absolute and eternal. Once we accept this truth, we are free to loose our fingers from the control of our lives and turn the helm over to Him. Because He is sovereign, we have sufficient basis for our complete surrender to Him.

CHAPTER FIVE

...And the Free Will of Man

There are two sides to the coin that's tossed in the air at the start of a football game—heads and tails. In like manner, there are two sides to God's relationship with man. On the one side we have God's sovereignty and on the flip side, the free will of man.

In our last chapter, we examined what scripture has to say about the sovereignty of God. Before we move forward in our study of full and unconditional surrender, we need to look also at what the Bible tells us about the flip side, the free choice of man. Without free choice, the issue of surrender is irrelevant. Without it, mankind is just a puppet with God pulling the strings. If man has no choice of his own then, there's nothing to surrender. Whatever God says, man would do. Nothing else. I confess, sometimes it seems that life would be a whole lot easier if things worked that way!

But God, in His sovereignty, chose to give us the right to choose, and in doing so He forces the issue of obedience out of the overflow of the heart. In other words, in giving man free choice, God is saying He wants voluntary submission as opposed to coerced law-keeping. There's quite a difference in the two.

Sovereignty First, Choice Second

It begins with the sovereignty of God. Then "free will" (or choice) is added to the mix. God created man and woman in His image, which means that at inception mankind was perfect in every way—just like God. Without the freedom to choose, mankind would have remained in that perfect state forever. But God, in His sovereignty, chose to allow man to think for himself and make his own decisions. At that point, the battle was on and it has lasted even until today.

We see it first in the garden of Eden. In Genesis Chapter 3, the serpent (identified as Satan according to Revelation 12:9, 20:2) confronts Eve with the option of choosing for herself what she wants to do. We established in earlier chapters that Satan cannot do anything without first getting God's permission, so we know he's not the one who initiates "choice." Here, he is merely using the choice God has already given to mankind. His plan is to tempt Eve to decide for Self against the will of God.

> **[1]Now the serpent was more crafty than any of the wild animals the Lord God had made. He said to the woman, "Did God really say, 'You must not eat from any tree in the garden'?"** [Genesis 3:1, NIV]

The first thing the serpent does is to create doubt. This is the common basis for all temptation—doubting the absolute truth of God's word, questioning His authority to set the parameters for our behavior, denying the timelessness of His word and subsequently negating its relevance to our lives today. The woman doesn't bite, however, but stands strong on the word of God. Let's look at her response.

> **²The woman said to the serpent, "We may
> eat fruit from the trees in the garden· ³but
> God did say, 'You must not eat fruit from
> the tree that is in the middle of the garden,
> and you must not touch it, or you will die.' "**
> [Genesis 3:2-3, NIV]

What parameters had God put on their behavior? What
limitation did Eve understand God to put on her and Adam's
freedom? It should be noted that God actually gave this
instruction to Adam (see Genesis 2:15-17) but apparently
Adam passed it on to his partner as she was aware of the
rules (even if she doesn't quote it exactly right). When she
confronts the serpent with the correct word of God, however,
he doesn't give up. Whereas at first he was merely casting
doubt, now he resorts to out-and-out lies.

> **⁴"You will not surely die," the serpent said
> to the woman. ⁵"For God knows that when
> you eat of it your eyes will be opened, and
> you will be like God, knowing good and
> evil."** [Genesis 3:4-5, NIV]

The ultimate temptation being offered to the woman
seems to be that of becoming equal to God. This is the
power trip many Christians find themselves on today. It's
called wanting to remain in control of our own lives. It was
something desirable to mankind in the beginning—it's just
as desirable to us today. Let's read on to see how the woman
handles the temptation Satan lays before her.

> **⁶When the woman saw that the fruit of
> the tree was good for food and pleasing
> to the eye, and also desirable for gaining
> wisdom, she took some and ate it. She also**

gave some to her husband, who was with her, and he ate it. ⁷Then the eyes of both of them were opened, and they realized they were naked; so they sewed fig leaves together and made coverings for themselves. [Genesis 3:6-7, NIV]

The first man and the first woman succumb to temptation when they indulge in the fruit of the tree of knowledge of good and evil. Even though God had given no explanation for placing the fruit of this tree off-limits, Satan made the claim that it would make them as wise as God. We cannot be sure, but perhaps that was the motivation behind their eating the fruit. (Scripture says simply that the woman saw that it was desirable for gaining wisdom.) That's not the main issue, though. The issue is the fact they disobeyed God. Satan had laid before them the option to please God or to please Self. And with the freedom of choice that God had given them, they chose to please Self.

Could God have kept His people perfect and free of sin forever? Absolutely! But in His sovereignty, God chose to give man the option to choose.

Between Blessings and Curses

We see this illustrated again in Deuteronomy 30:15-20. In preceding chapters, God has laid out for the children of Israel a list of blessings that are theirs if they obey and a list of curses that are theirs if they disobey. After presenting the two lists, here is what God says:

¹⁵See, I set before you today life and prosperity, death and destruction. ¹⁶For I command you today to love the Lord your

God, to walk in his ways, and to keep his commands, decrees and laws; then you will live and increase, and the Lord your God will bless you in the land you are entering to possess.

[17]But if your heart turns away and you are not obedient, and if you are drawn away to bow down to other gods and worship them, [18]I declare to you this day that you will certainly be destroyed. You will not live long in the land you are crossing the Jordan to enter and possess.

[19]This day I call heaven and earth as witnesses against you that I have set before you life and death, blessings and curses. Now choose life, so that you and your children may live [20]and that you may love the Lord your God, listen to his voice, and hold fast to him. For the Lord is your life, and he will give you many years in the land he swore to give to your fathers, Abraham, Isaac and Jacob. [Deuteronomy 30:15-20, NIV]

In verses 15-16, God tells the Israelites that He has set a choice before them: obey or disobey. In verse 16, then, He promises blessings to those who obey, and in verses 17-18 He promises destruction to those who disobey. In God's eyes the choice between obedience and disobedient, blessings and curses, life and death are all the same. What does God desire for us? He states it clearly in the last part of verse 19: "Now choose life, so that you and your children may live." And then in verse 20, He clarifies what is meant by the term "life." "The Lord is your life." In essence, then, God is telling us to choose Him.

That's God's desire for us. He doesn't want any to be lost but all to come to repentance. He wants everyone to obey, He wants everyone to live, He wants everyone to come to Him. Yet... in His sovereignty God chose to give everyone the right to choose for himself. He wants us to come to Him because we *want* to, not because there's no other option available to us.

The children of Israel chose to disobey God and follow the desires of their own heart. As a result they wandered in the wilderness for forty years until every sinful adult had been purged from their midst. Since God is the God who is, was and always shall be, can we expect anything less today? It's a timeless teaching: obedience to God brings blessing; disobedience, curses. He doesn't promise a life free of troubles or concerns, but He does promise a life filled with joy and an after-life wholly and completely free of trouble, concern, pain, tears... you name it. Nothing unpleasant will be in heaven for those who choose to obey God rather than Self.

Salvation and the Issue of "Free Choice"

A specific area of "man's free choice" is addressed in the New Testament and that's in the area of salvation. This is another of those oft-debated questions: Is salvation the result of God's election or man's free choice? For a short while here, let's ignore what we know from denominational teachings and go straight to the Word of God.

First of all, we need to note that when it comes to the issue of salvation, way too many people stand in one of two opposing camps—either claiming that God *alone* makes the choice or that man *alone* does. According to 2 Timothy 3:16 all scripture is God-breathed—all scripture comes out of the mouth of God and is therefore truth—and so, however we interpret scripture we must not deny either of the two truths it teaches on the subject: (1) God chooses; and (2) Man chooses.

In John 15:16a, we hear Jesus say, "You did not choose me, but I chose you..." And then again in verse 19, "...I chose you out of the world." In the short span of just four verses Jesus tells us twice. When God repeats Himself like this, He wants us to get the point. So what's the point He's making? That it is through the sovereign election of God that we are saved.

We get a little confused about this sometimes and tend to think we have something to do with it. In Ephesians 2:8, Paul puts it like this: "For it is by grace you have been saved... and this not from yourselves, it is the gift of God—not by works..." I don't think He could make it any clearer: God's grace, not man's efforts, desires or will, is what saves us. In John 6:44a, Jesus states the same thing in another way: "No one can come to me unless the Father who sent me draws him..." And then there's Romans 8:29 in which Paul tells us that those "whom God foreknew, He also predestined to be conformed to the likeness of His Son." In all of this, we see that there is a crucial role that the Father plays in the salvation process. He's the One who initiates everything; He chooses and He draws people to Him through Jesus. And He makes it clear that they are not coming to Him by any other means than the "election of God"!

Yet (and that's a very big "yet") scripture also says, "...to all who received him, to those who believed in his name, he gave the right to become children of God." [John 1:12, NIV] According to this passage, to whom does God give the right to become His? To *all* who receive Him and who believe in His name. What's this saying to us? That those who acknowledge Jesus' claims and believe what He says have the opportunity to become a child of God... to be saved. John 3:16 puts it in a very similar way: "...whoever believes in Him should not perish but have eternal life." That means everyone who chooses on his own volition to do so. Again, there is a choice involved on the part of man *in addition* to the sovereign act of God. God chooses, but man must decide to yield to the sovereign Lord.

We cannot be dogmatic about any position, but it may be that God's foreknowledge is the key to our understanding this apparent dichotomy in scripture. God is omniscient. This means He knows all things—*even* before anything happens (i.e., He has foreknowledge). If God knows ahead of time everyone who is going to decide for Him, doesn't it make sense that these would be the ones He draws to Him? This may not be the perfect answer, but it does explain one way in which both Election and Free Will can be involved in the salvation process, as scripture plainly states they are. In other words, God's teachings on sovereignty must always be considered in light of the opposite; that is, His teachings on the free will of man.

Choice Makes Surrender Necessary

It's because we have a choice (free will) that we find ourselves in a position in which we must surrender. As long as we're choosing in favor of our own desires, that need will exist. Only as we empty ourselves of selfish desires and endeavor to do everything God wants us to do will we be completely in the will of God. And that of course is the very definition of surrender.

Surrender, then, is the ultimate goal of every true believer.

CHAPTER SIX

Taking Grace Into Consideration

We might ask at this point: "Where does the grace of God fit into all this?" Up to now, we've been talking about all we have to do if ever we're going to be able to loose our grip on our personal lives and turn everything over to God. We've learned that we have to fear Him, trust Him, and acknowledge His sovereignty over the universe in general and over our lives in particular. These are absolutes—fear, trust, acknowledgment of His sovercignty—without any one of them we would be unlikely to succeed in surrendering control of our lives to Him.

Once all three of these are firmly embedded in our life-style, however, there's a final element that serves as the catalyst to trigger surrender. We took a first glimpse at it in the previous chapter when we looked at Ephesians 2:8-9. In those verses, God makes it plain that we are saved by grace. In other words, there's nothing we can do to earn salvation; there's nothing we've ever done, or can do in the future, to deserve it. Human effort is out of the mix altogether. Salvation is a free gift, an act of grace that's initiated by God—not us.

This is the final element we must add to the mix: our coming to the realization that it's only because of God that we are saved. Here in Chapter 6, we'll spend a little time delving into the subject of grace and then go on to explore the demands its reality places on our lives. As in previous chapters, the Word of God is the only resource we will use as a reference.

Salvation by Grace in the Old Testament

If anyone had asked me a while back, I would have insisted that "grace" was a New Testament concept. Much to my surprise, a search of an exhaustive concordance reveals that the English word "grace" occurs eight times in the Old Testament (New International Version). Eight isn't a whole lot when compared to the 122 times it appears in the New Testament, but the fact that the subject comes up at all is significant to the Bible student. Not that the Old Testament actually teaches salvation by grace, but it definitely points to the birth, death, resurrection and ascension of Jesus Christ, which we know is how the New Testament spells out salvation for the believer. Let's take a look at what Zechariah Chapter 12 has to say.

> [1]**This is the word of the Lord concerning Israel. The Lord, who stretches out the heavens, who lays the foundation of the earth, and who forms the spirit of man within him, declares:** [2] **"I am going to make Jerusalem a cup that sends all the surrounding peoples reeling. Judah will be besieged as well as Jerusalem.** [3]**On that day, when all the nations of the earth are gathered against her, I will make Jerusalem an immovable rock for all the nations. All who try to move it will injure themselves.**

⁴On that day I will strike every horse with panic and its rider with madness," declares the Lord. "I will keep a watchful eye over the house of Judah, but I will blind all the horses of the nations. ⁵Then the leaders of Judah will say in their hearts, 'The people of Jerusalem are strong, because the Lord Almighty is their God.'

⁶"On that day I will make the leaders of Judah like a firepot in a woodpile, like a flaming torch among sheaves. They will consume right and left all the surrounding peoples, but Jerusalem will remain intact in her place.

⁷"The Lord will save the dwellings of Judah first, so that the honor of the house of David and of Jerusalem's inhabitants may not be greater than that of Judah. ⁸On that day the Lord will shield those who live in Jerusalem, so that the feeblest among them will be like David, and the house of David will be like God, like the Angel of the Lord going before them. [9] On that day I will set out to destroy all the nations that attack Jerusalem.

¹⁰"And I will pour out on the house of David and the inhabitants of Jerusalem a spirit of grace and supplication. They will look on me, the one they have pierced, and they will mourn for him as one mourns for an only child, and grieve bitterly for him as

one grieves for a firstborn son." [Zechariah
12:1-10, NIV]

After you've read the passage once, go back and read it
a second time. On the second run-through, mark the phrase
"on that day" with its own identifying symbol using pen,
highlight, or colored pencil. After you finish, we'll tackle
the question, "To what time period does the phrase 'on that
day' refer?"

We find the answer to our question in verse 2 which tells
us the Lord is "...going to make Jerusalem a cup that sends
all the surrounding peoples reeling," and that Judah "will
be besieged." These are actually two separate prophecies—
we'll begin with the second one.

Zechariah prophesied during the days *following* Judah's
exile to Babylon and her return, so the reference here to an
attack against Judah ("Judah will be besieged") obviously
does *not* refer to its capture by Babylon. Neither has there
been a time since Zechariah's writing the book during which
"all the nations of the earth" have gathered against Jerusalem
as verse 3 tells us they will do. Yet... if God says these two
things are going to happen and they haven't happened yet,
we know they will happen at some point down the road. So,
when Zechariah uses the phrase "on that day," we can determine that it is referring to a time still future to us today.

Now let's look closer at what is going to happen on that
day. According to verses 2 & 3, Jerusalem (and Judah) is
going to be attacked by *all* the nations of the earth. When
she is attacked, God will cause her to become a "cup," an
"immoveable rock," that He will use to bring destruction
on all her attackers. At that time, Jerusalem (Judah) will
be victorious against the entire world, and God will put
a "spirit of grace and supplication" into the hearts of the
entire Jewish nation.

When we read the phrase "a spirit of grace and suppli-cation," what appears to be the implication? The definition seems to be found in the second half of the verse. It's telling us that a "spirit of grace and supplication" is given when the Jews look to Jesus (the One whom they rejected and cruci-fied) in faith at the Second Advent. This is an obvious refer-ence to salvation. Bottom line then, Zechariah is teaching salvation by grace for the Jews. Because Christ is the only way to the Father (according to John 14:6) and He had not yet come at the time of the writing, the prophet must have been referring to a future time when the Jewish nation will be saved by faith through Jesus Christ. We've already estab-lished that that time is still future to us today.

Now read Galatians 3:8.

> **"The Scripture foresaw that God would justify the Gentiles by faith, and announced the gospel in advance to Abraham: 'All nations will be blessed through you.' "**
> [NIV]

The gospel is the story of how God the Son came to earth to live as a man, yet to remain without sin; who took upon Himself the sins of the world; and suffered death on the cross so that everyone who believes in Him might have eternal life. This is the message that Galatians 3:8 tells us was announced to Abraham at the time he was called by God to leave his country and go to a place where God would send him. (The phrase "All nations will be blessed through you" in Galatians 3:8 refers us back to Genesis 12:1-3 and the calling of Abraham as father of all God's people.)

Conclusion? The Old Testament teaches salvation by grace just as the New Testament does. God's teaching is consistent throughout the Bible: we are saved, not because of any merit we might have, but because of His mercy and the love that He has for the unlovable.

The Hugeness of Grace in the New Testament

Just how big is this "grace" that God bestowed upon us in order to save us? Let's take a closer look.

From Romans 3:23, we learn that we've all sinned and fall short of the glory of God. Then in Romans 6:23, we see that the natural consequences of this sin is death. For the full impact of the kind of "death" sin brings about, we look to Lazarus and the rich man in Luke 16 below.

> [19]"There was a rich man who was dressed in purple and fine linen and lived in luxury every day. [20]At his gate was laid a beggar named Lazarus, covered with sores [21]and longing to eat what fell from the rich man's table. Even the dogs came and licked his sores.
>
> [22]"The time came when the beggar died and the angels carried him to Abraham's side. The rich man also died and was buried. [23]In hell, where he was in torment, he looked up and saw Abraham far away, with Lazarus by his side. [24]So he called to him, 'Father Abraham, have pity on me and send Lazarus to dip the tip of his finger in water and cool my tongue, because I am in agony in this fire.'
>
> [25]"But Abraham replied, 'Son, remember that in your lifetime you received your good

things, while Lazarus received bad things, but now he is comforted here and you are in agony. ²⁶And besides all this, between us and you a great chasm has been fixed, so that those who want to go from here to you cannot, nor can anyone cross over from there to us.'

²⁷"He answered, 'Then I beg you, father, send Lazarus to my father's house, ²⁸for I have five brothers. Let him warn them, so that they will not also come to this place of torment.'

²⁹"Abraham replied, 'They have Moses and the Prophets; let them listen to them.'

³⁰" 'No, father Abraham,' he said, 'but if someone from the dead goes to them, they will repent.'

³¹"He said to him, 'If they do not listen to Moses and the Prophets, they will not be convinced even if someone rises from the dead.' " [Luke 16:19-31, NIV]

The key is found in verses 23 through 26. According to verse 23, the rich man is "far away" from Lazarus and Father Abraham in heaven. We see that Lazarus is being comforted there while the rich man is being tormented in hell. Verse 26 tells us that there is a great chasm separating hell and the place where Lazarus rests. This is the picture that God gave to show us how sin separates us from Him. This means, then, that the "death" referred to in Romans 6:23 ("...the wages of

77

sin is death") is more than just physical death; it is an eternity of existence outside the presence of God.

But in His grace—not because of anything we have done, but only because of Who He is—God sent His Son to die in our stead. He made Him Who had no sin to be sin for us so that we might become the righteousness of God (2 Corinthians 5:21). And He did this, according to Romans 5:8, "...while we were still sinners." Obviously, if we were still sinners, there is no way we could have deserved the reconciliation Jesus brought about through His sacrifice because the "wages of sin is death."

Bottom line, our undeserved, unmerited, unearned salvation cost Jesus His life. His sacrifice for our sins came at the expense of an agony so great the Bible describes Him as "sweating something like drops of blood" while praying in the Garden of Gethsemane (Luke 22:39-46). Crucifixion was the most grisly of all executions; death coming typically only after a long period of excruciating pain—usually days. But for Jesus, the pain was even greater as He knew His execution meant separation from God the Father.

This is the price our Lord paid for the atonement of our sins. Our salvation comes at His great cost. The size of His gift is immeasurable. It is non-repayable.

Grace Demands Surrender

The point being is this: His gift to us is so immense our only appropriate response is to give our lives right back to Him. Anything less minimizes the magnitude of the sacrifice He made for us. Anything less is our failure to recognize the enormity of God's grace on our behalf.

Bottom line—grace demands surrender.

Part II

What Surrender Looks Like

CHAPTER SEVEN 7

Presenting Your Body

In previous chapters we've established the fact that we must fear God, we must trust Him, we must acknowledge in our hearts that He is in control of all things, and that in His sovereignty He gives man a choice in the matters before him. Then in Chapter 6, we looked at the role God plays in our salvation and acknowledged Him as the initiator. In other words, it's not what we do that earns us our salvation, it's the grace of God. As we read in the last paragraph of Chapter 6, the enormity of God's grace makes our only appropriate response to be one of surrender to Him. In its simplest form, surrender is the most *natural* of all things for us to do.

That raises the question: "What does the surrendered life look like?" If we're supposed to surrender to Him, we need to know what that surrendered life entails. This chapter addresses that question, as does the rest of the book.

A Spiritual Act of Worship

In his letter to the believers in Rome, Paul gives insight into what the surrendered life is like. Let's begin with Romans 12:1-2.

[1]Therefore, I urge you, brothers, in view of
God's mercy, to offer your bodies as living
sacrifices, holy and pleasing to God—this
is your spiritual act of worship. [2] Do not
conform any longer to the pattern of this
world, but be transformed by the renewing
of your mind. Then you will be able to test
and approve what God's will is—his good,
pleasing and perfect will. [Romans 12:1-2
NIV]

There are several words within the text that are key to our
understanding. The first one is the word "spiritual" in verse
1. This verse reads: "This is your spiritual act of worship."
Obviously, we need to know what "this" is; in other words,
how is "a spiritual act of worship" defined.

If we were to read the same text in different translations,
we would see different English words used to translate the
original Greek. Where the New International Version says
"spiritual," the King James Version uses the word "reasonable," the New American Standard Bible says "acceptable,"
and the New Living Translation refers to an act of worship
(sacrifice) as being "the kind He will accept." The Greek
word that's translated in such different ways is *logikos*.

Let's look at that word *logikos*. Our first impression of
the word might be to associate it with the Greek word *logos*,
translated by the English equivalent, "word." Or our thoughts
might even take us to the English word "logical." If we look
logikos up in a Greek dictionary, we see that it means "of
the word, rational, logical"—pretty much what we'd expect
from just a cursory observation of the word. Plugging the
new understanding back into our text in Romans 12:1, we see
that we are to present our bodies to Him as our *reasonable,
rational, acceptable* act of worship. Makes a lot of sense,
doesn't it? Especially in light of what we've been studying

up to this point—that in light of God's grace and mercies towards us, surrender is the only appropriate response; it's our natural response; it's our *reasonable* response.

"Offer Your Bodies..."

Another important word from our Romans 12:1-2 text is the Greek word that's translated in the NIV as "offer." The text reads, "...offer your bodies as a living sacrifice" in verse 1. What does it mean to "offer"?

The Greek here is *paristemi*. This word is a combination of two Greek words: *para* and *histemi*. The Greek *histemi* means to stand; and *para* means *near, in the vicinity of* or in *proximity* with. Put them together and we have the idea of "standing beside." With this word, God is painting a picture for us of what "offering" our bodies is all about. By instructing us to offer our bodies to Him, He's telling us to get those bodies from "here"—where we are now—to "there" where He is! In other words, to turn them over to Him, to relinquish them from under our control to under His.

One of the fascinating realities about the Bible is how other scriptures help clarify what we don't fully understand in the particular text we're reading. Let's take a look at another scripture that's closely related to this thought of "offering" our bodies; this one also from the book of Romans.

> **Do not offer the parts of your body to sin, as instruments of wickedness, but rather offer yourselves to God, as those who have been brought from death to life; and offer the parts of your body to him as instruments of righteousness.** [Romans 6:13, NIV]

If we focus in on the last two-thirds of the verse, we see that we are to offer our bodies to God... and we're to do it as one who has been brought back *from death to life*. Again, we see that connection with the bottom line of Chapter 6. Through His grace (and His grace alone) God brought us to salvation; in other words, He brought us from death to life. So when Paul says in Romans 6:13 that we are to offer our bodies to God as one who has been brought from death to life, we know he's making a reference to God's grace. Our reasonable response to God's grace is our surrender. It all ties together so beautifully.

A second point that Paul makes here: we are to offer our bodies to God as *instruments of righteousness*. Apparently "offering our bodies as living sacrifices" means giving all of ourselves to Him for His use (and hence, the reference to "instruments of righteousness"). God is righteousness so the only way we can be "instruments of righteousness" would be for Him to be working through us. And in order for that to happen, we must first give our bodies to Him. It's as simple as that.

Conformed and Transformed

At this point, we're ready to go back to the print-out of Romans 12:1-2 located near the front of the chapter. There are two additional words from the passage that we want to understand before moving on.

As we re-read the passage, let's pay special attention to verse 2. God's penman Paul gives two imperatives in this verse. First of all, we are to "not be conformed" and secondly, we are to "be transformed." The Greek word *suschematizo* translated "conformed" here carries the idea of fashioning ones self according to another. In other words, God is telling us in no uncertain terms that we are not to fashion ourselves after the world and what it does, but we are to be "transformed." And the Greek word translated "transformed" is *metamorphoo*, meaning to change or to metamorphose. Webster defines "metamorphose" as changing into a different physical form especially by supernatural means; or to change strikingly the appearance or character of something. Bottom line, we are not to be like the world in what we do, say and think; but we are to change supernaturally into something quite different—both in appearance and in character.

How do we go about accomplishing such a metamorphosis as God is commanding? In Matthew 12:34 Jesus tells us that "Out of the overflow of the heart, the mouth speaks." And Paul says in Philippians 4:8: "...whatever is true, whatever is noble, whatever is right, whatever is pure, whatever is lovely, whatever is admirable—if anything is excellent or praiseworthy—think about such things." In other words, as we feed our minds with the good and godly things, our hearts are transformed likewise. Rather than continuing as the world does, we set our sights on God and walk according to His flight plan and not our own.

Dead to Sin, Alive to Christ

Earlier we looked at verse 13 of Romans Chapter 6. Now let's go back and look further at the rest of the chapter. As you read the text printed out for you below, circle or highlight every reference to death, dying and all synonyms.

> **[1]What shall we say, then? Shall we go on sinning so that grace may increase? [2]By no means! We died to sin; how can we live in it any longer? [3]Or don't you know that all of us who were baptized into Christ Jesus were baptized into his death? [4]We were**

therefore buried with him through baptism into death in order that, just as Christ was raised from the dead through the glory of the Father, we too may live a new life.

⁵If we have been united with him like this in his death, we will certainly also be united with him in his resurrection. ⁶For we know that our old self was crucified with him so that the body of sin might be done away with, that we should no longer be slaves to sin— ⁷because anyone who has died has been freed from sin.

⁸Now if we died with Christ, we believe that we will also live with him. ⁹For we know that since Christ was raised from the dead, he cannot die again; death no longer has mastery over him. ¹⁰The death he died, he died to sin once for all; but the life he lives, he lives to God.

¹¹In the same way, count yourselves dead to sin but alive to God in Christ Jesus. ¹²Therefore do not let sin reign in your mortal body so that you obey its evil desires. ¹³Do not offer the parts of your body to sin, as instruments of wickedness, but rather offer yourselves to God, as those who have been brought from death to life; and offer the parts of your body to him as instruments of righteousness. ¹⁴For sin shall not be your master, because you are not under law, but under grace.

¹⁵What then? Shall we sin because we are not under law but under grace? By no means! ¹⁶Don't you know that when you offer yourselves to someone to obey him as slaves, you are slaves to the one whom you obey—whether you are slaves to sin, which leads to death, or to obedience, which leads to righteousness? ¹⁷But thanks be to God that, though you used to be slaves to sin, you wholeheartedly obeyed the form of teaching to which you were entrusted. ¹⁸You have been set free from sin and have become slaves to righteousness.

¹⁹I put this in human terms because you are weak in your natural selves. Just as you used to offer the parts of your body in slavery to impurity and to ever-increasing wickedness, so now offer them in slavery to righteousness leading to holiness. ²⁰When you were slaves to sin, you were free from the control of righteousness. ²¹What benefit did you reap at that time from the things you are now ashamed of? Those things result in death! ²²But now that you have been set free from sin and have become slaves to God, the benefit you reap leads to holiness, and the result is eternal life. ²³For the wages of sin is death, but the gift of God is eternal life in Christ Jesus our Lord. [Romans 6, NIV]

Notice the terminology Paul uses in the passage. As we observe the references to death, dying and their synonyms, we see that we have died to a particular condition. Let's look at those references.

We have our first reference in verse 2: "We died to sin." In verse 3 we have a reference to our being baptized into Jesus' death; in other words, we are crucified with Him "so that the body of sin might be done away with" and we are "no longer slaves to sin" (v.6). We are "freed from sin" according to verse 7. Then in verse 11, in the same way Christ died to sin, we are to "count ourselves dead to sin." There are additional references in verses 17, 18, 20, 22 that make the reference to our once being slaves to sin and now we are no more. According to what Paul is saying here, we cannot escape the fact that we have died to the control sin once had over us.

Okay then, if we've died to the control of sin over our lives, what are we living for? We find the answer in verses 8 and 11: we live with Christ and are alive to God in Him. If we are dead to sin and alive to Christ, then, isn't it reasonable we would no longer offer our body parts to sin? To give oneself to sin would be analogous to being alive to sin and Paul has already established the fact that we are dead to sin. And once again we see that surrendering to God is our only reasonable action.

Slaves to the One You Obey

From verse 16, we pick up on another key thought: "Don't you know that when you offer yourselves to someone to obey him as slaves, you are slaves to the one whom you obey whether you are slaves to sin, which leads to death, or to obedience, which leads to righteousness?" This word "slave" or "slavery" appears nine times in the passage between verses 15 and 23. Paul says we're either a slave to sin or a slave to obedience—it's one or the other; there's no gray in between. It's absolute. Yet we know we cannot be a slave to sin because Paul goes to great lengths to show that we are dead to sin. That means we must be slaves to obedience that leads to righteousness and so we must give our bodies over to righteousness. This is just one more time we see that our only reasonable response seems to be the surrender of our bodies to God.

It's interesting to note the meaning of the word that's translated "slave" in the passage above. The Greek word *doulos* can refer to either a voluntary or involuntary situation and can be translated either "slave" or "servant." But even when voluntary, the slave/servant cannot leave whenever he desires as the translation "servant" might imply. The word *doulos* is derived from the Greek *deo* which means to bind. A servant who is "bound" to his master cannot take leave of his master even if it is called voluntary. Plugging this back into our text at Romans 6:15-23, we see that if we are a slave to obedience which leads to righteousness, we are bound to that obedience and righteousness. It is our life-style forever.

As a servant—*doulos*—of God today, the words "No, Lord" are eliminated from our thoughts and replaced automatically with "Yes, Lord" in everything that comes our way. If He is our master (and that's exactly what the word "Lord" means), then our only response to everything He asks of us must be a resounding "yes."

No matter how we look at the subject, we eventually come full circle to the realization that if we love Jesus, we will surrender our will to His and do whatever we can to continue walking in His ways.

Developing a Picture of the Surrendered Life

Our discussion here in Chapter 7 is just the beginning of a picture we're developing about what the surrendered life looks like. We'll take it a step further in Chapter 8 as we examine what Jesus means in regards to laying down our lives.

CHAPTER EIGHT

Laying Down Your Life

In the previous chapter we looked at the command God gives through His servant Paul that we offer our bodies to Him as a living sacrifice (Romans 12:1-2). We are empowered to do this, Paul tells us earlier in Romans Chapter 6, through our death to sin and the fact that we now live for Christ.

In the current chapter, we continue along the same line—dying to sin and living for Christ—but this time we'll view it from the perspective of Jesus' teaching in John 15:13: "Greater love has no one than this, that he lay down his life for his friends."

No Greater Love Than This

This is an interesting thought. What Jesus is telling us in John 15:13 is that the greatest means we have for showing our love to our friends is the act of laying down our life for them. Often when we read this verse, we assume that the phrase "laying down our life" means that we are willing to die for another person. After all, that's what Jesus did when he laid down His life for us. The connection is tightly woven in scripture. In 1 John 3:16, the author puts it this way: "This

is how we know what love is: Jesus Christ laid down His life
for us. And we ought to lay down our lives for our brothers."
We see the connection plainly here: in the manner in which
Jesus laid down His life, we ought to lay down ours. In other
words, we are to be willing to die for our fellow Christians
just as Jesus died for us on the cross. This is all very true, but
it is not the complete picture.

The Connection Between Death and a Living Sacrifice

If we read the command of John 15:13 in light of what
we've learned previously in Romans 12:1-2, "laying down
our lives" takes on new meaning. Here's the simple truth of
the matter: Jesus does not ask you to die for Him but to lay
down your life for Him. He's not asking for a "dead" sacrifice; He's asking for a living one just as Paul describes it in
Romans Chapter 12:1-2.

Yes, Jesus died a physical death on the cross in order to
give us life, and we might one day be called to die for the
cause as well. But Jesus did more than just die. He suffered.
After emptying Himself of all that He was as God and taking
on the very nature of human likeness (Philippians 2:5-11), He
submitted Himself to the humiliation, agony, and shame of
all that led up to the cross—all three years of it. Throughout
His entire ministry He subjected Himself to the will of the
Father. This is exactly what He calls you and me to do.

Before you heave a sigh of relief that the John 15:13
passage is not necessarily calling you to die for someone,
think about what it means to "lay down your life." It is much
easier, I believe, to die a physical death than to lay down
your life day in and day out. Dying is a one-time event;
laying down your life is an ongoing, continuous action that
involves emptying yourself of all that you believe, do, have
and will ever become. There is nothing easy about it.

Living Sacrifice Can Be More Difficult

Let's think a minute about Peter's comments to Jesus after Jesus told the disciples that He was going away and they were not going to be able to follow until later. What was Peter's response? "Lord, why can't I follow you now? I will lay down my life for you." To which Jesus replies, "Will you really lay down your life for me?"

What if Jesus were to ask you that same question? Most of us are quick to pay lip-service to a willingness to put Jesus first, but the question is: "Will you *really* lay down your life for Jesus?" Will you deny yourself the comforts of home and take up His burden? Will you endure rejection and ridicule for His name's sake and continue to stand boldly on His promises? Are you willing to forsake the ways of the world and walk in the light by faith, and by faith alone? We're not talking about dying a physical death here; we're talking about giving up things we consider rightfully ours in order to give Him top priority in our lives.

As much as Peter loved Jesus, Peter was quick to fall away. Just as Jesus had predicted he would, the rooster had not crowed even once before Peter had already denied knowing Jesus—not once but three times. Peter had sworn it would never happen; he believed that it wouldn't. But it did. Three times. Many of us do not walk nearly so close to Jesus as Peter did. How much suffering would it take before we would turn our back to Him and pursue the ways of the world? It's a question each of us needs to answer for himself: "How much would it take to lure me away?"

Several years ago, I received a letter from a Messianic Jew—we'll call him Avram for the purpose of this writing. Avram's ex-wife had recently passed away and left their two pre-teen sons to live with her parents, the boys' grandparents. Since the divorce years before, the boys' mother had poisoned their minds against their father, even blaming the break-up on him rather than admitting that she had run off with another man. During their growing-up years, the boys had not been allowed to see or to talk with their father. Now that their mother was gone, they were choosing to live with the maternal grandparents and refusing even to talk with their father during the custody battle that ensued. Avram faced a tough decision: he could share the truth about his ex-wife and their break-up with his sons—this might help them to forgive him but would risk destroying their good memory of their mother—or he could remain silent. Avram agonized over the reality of losing his sons if he didn't speak up but eventually his love for the boys won out. He remained silent and the court awarded custody of the boys to their grandparents. Avram lost all parental rights.

Sometimes the right thing to do is to let go. Despite the pain such a decision entailed for Avram, the happiness of his sons meant more to him than his own. This is a good example of "laying down your life" for someone you love. Avram didn't die a physical death. Instead, he was to face the pain of losing his sons over and over every day for the rest of his life. I'm sure Avram would be the first to tell you that dying a physical death would have been a whole lot easier.

Called to Lay Down Your Life

Jesus calls us to lay down our lives for others. That's what He says in John 15:13. "Greater love has no one than this, that he lay down his life for his friends." It's not an easy assignment, but one that requires continuous discipline and dedication. Jesus never promised it would be easy.

But this is what Jesus did and it's what He calls the surrendered believer to do.

CHAPTER NINE

Giving It All to God in Prayer

How important would you say prayer is in your life? Personally, I'd be hard-pressed for an answer to a question like that; I think most true believers would be. Let's give it a shot. For starters, prayer is our life. It's our breath, it's our direction. Our rest, our inspiration, our comfort. Bottom line, no matter how we look at it, prayer is *everything* to the Christian.

Anything as important as this is obviously going to have a lot of books written about it and a lot of teaching and preaching done on the subject. Peruse through the books on the shelves at your local Christian bookstore and you'll find "how-to"s galore. Everyone seems to have a marketable theory on how to make prayer work better for you.

Herein lies the problem.

We Don't Make Prayer Work for Us

We don't *make* prayer work for us. Prayer is a conversation with God. There can be no rules, formats, formulas or the like. Prayer is what God wants it to be and not what man says it should be. Prayer is the natural outcome of a relationship that's shared between us and God. It is an expression of love that ceases to be love once we reduce it to the mechanical.

We want to keep this in mind as we continue through the chapter. You may have already noticed that our chapter title has nothing to do with the mechanics of prayer but states simply that we are to give it all to God in prayer. That's the approach we take in this chapter—submitting all that we are to Him, surrendering completely to His will, once again being "out of control and lovin' every minute of it."

Prayer and surrender are inseparable. To have prayer without surrender is flat wrong; surrender without prayer, an impossibility. That's the hypothesis for this chapter; the proof is found in scripture.

"Thy Will Be Done..."

We'll start with a passage you're probably familiar with—the Lord's Prayer as given to us in Matthew 6:9-13. But before we look at that text, we need to set its context by reading the parallel account in Luke chapter 11.

> **One day Jesus was praying in a certain place. When he finished, one of his disciples said to him, "Lord, teach us to pray, just as John taught his disciples. He said to them, "When you pray, say: 'Father, hallowed be your name, your kingdom come. Give us each day our daily bread. Forgive us our sins, for we also forgive everyone who sins against us. And lead us not into temptation.'"** [Luke 11:1-4, NIV]

We see from verse 1 that Jesus' disciples asked him to teach them how to pray. They lived with Jesus day in and day out; they had witnessed up-close and personal His relationship with the Father and they knew that prayer played a vital role in His daily life. Undoubtedly, He had prayed with them many times and they recognized a special power He had in regards to prayer.

Jesus' response to the disciples' request may sound familiar to you. The words are not exactly the same, but the substance is definitely there. The prayer is a rendition of the one we've come to call "The Lord's Prayer." Most of us are probably more familiar with the way it's worded in the Matthew account, particularly in the King James translation; so that's the one we'll look at.

> **After this manner therefore pray ye: Our Father which art in heaven, Hallowed be thy name. Thy kingdom come. Thy will be done in earth, as it is in heaven. Give us this day our daily bread. And forgive us our debts, as we forgive our debtors. And lead us not into temptation, but deliver us from evil: For thine is the kingdom, and the power, and the glory, for ever. Amen.**
> [Matthew 6:9b-13, KJV]

Jesus introduces this prayer with the phrase "after this manner therefore pray ye." These words are in response to the disciple's request in Luke 11:1 that Jesus teach them how to pray. In the New International Version (NIV) His response reads, "This, then, is how you should pray." The prayer He gives following these words is therefore a model for our use whenever we pray—every time we pray. It's not necessary to use the exact same words. We can pray effectively by using the thoughts behind the words Jesus gives us here.

Look, then, at verse 10: "Thy will be done in earth, as it is in heaven." What is this saying to us? Hopefully, we

should be able to hear the submission this verse contains—
the surrender of our will to His. And we should be reminded
of Jesus' prayer in the Garden of Gethsemane that we studied
back in Chapter 1. Jesus prayed that God would take the cup
from Him; but hastened to add, "...yet not my will, but yours
be done." Back there, we saw that Jesus was agonizing over
the cup; yet regardless of the extent of His dread, of more
importance to Him was His carrying out the will of God.

Your Attitude Should Be the Same as Christ's

In other words, Jesus prayed according to the will of
God. Then in the second chapter of Paul's letter to the church
at Philippi, we read:

> **Your attitude should be the same as that of
> Christ Jesus:**
> **Who, being in very nature God, did not
> consider equality with God something to be
> grasped, but made himself nothing, taking
> the very nature of a servant, being made
> in human likeness. And being found in
> appearance as a man, he humbled himself
> and became obedient to death—even death
> on a cross!** [Philippians 2:5-8, NIV]

We looked at this earlier, but let's look at that first line
again. "Your attitude should be the same as that of Christ
Jesus..." If Jesus prayed for God's will to be done rather
than His own, then we are to pray in that manner as well.
That means there's kind of a double whammy going on here.
In the "Lord's Prayer" Jesus instructs us to pray according to
God's will and then by example He shows us in the Garden
of Gethsemane that that is the way He prays and there-

fore it is the way we are to pray. There's no escaping the teaching we're getting here. When we pray, we are to submit totally, completely, in-our-entirety to God. We are to empty ourselves of all that we are and give ourselves over to God. This is an absolute.

Praying As Jesus Would Pray

The Apostle John spells it out for us both in his Gospel and in the first of his three letters: I've listed these references for your convenience below:

> **This is the confidence we have in approaching God: that if we ask anything according to His will, He hears us. And if we know that He hears us—whatever we ask—we know that we have what we asked of Him.** [1 John 5:14-15 NIV]

> **If you remain in me and my words remain in you, ask whatever you wish, and it will be given you.** [John 15:7, NIV]

> **Dear friends, if our hearts do not condemn us, we have confidence before God [22] and receive from him anything we ask, because we obey his commands and do what pleases him.** [1 John 3:21-22, NIV]

> **You may ask me for anything in my name, and I will do it.** [John 14:14, NIV]

What we want to observe in each of these passages is the condition God places on our prayers if we are to have a confidence that they will be answered. According to the first verse above (1 John 5:14-15), we are to pray according to the will of God. And whenever we pray according to the will of God, the scriptures tell us we will receive whatever it is that we are praying for. This is a promise and God's promises are always accomplished.

We learn also from John 15:7 that our prayers are answered if we remain in Jesus and His words remain in us. We might need to reason our way through this one a little. If we are in Jesus and His words are in us, what do you suppose we might say about our wants, desires, wishes? If we are truly in Him and His words in us, all our desires line up with His—and we would actually be praying according to His will and not our own.

Looking at the third reference above (1 John 3:21-22), we see that our prayers are answered when we obey His commands and do what pleases Him. What can this possibly mean other than "our doing His will." Once again, it appears obvious that we are talking about the same thing as the preceding verses. It all fits together so easily.

Now let's look at the last verse (John 14:14). The wording is a little different here: "in His name" rather than "according to His will." Perhaps you see the connection immediately, but not everyone will so let's give it a closer look.

We can learn a lot from the use of the same phrase in 1 Kings 21 (printed out for you below).

Some time later there was an incident involving a vineyard belonging to Naboth the Jezreelite. The vineyard was in Jezreel, close to the palace of Ahab king of Samaria. Ahab said to Naboth, "Let me have your vineyard to use for a vegetable garden, since it is close to my palace. In exchange I will give you a better vineyard

or, if you prefer, I will pay you whatever it is worth."

But Naboth replied, "The Lord forbid that I should give you the inheritance of my fathers."

So Ahab went home, sullen and angry because Naboth the Jezreelite had said, "I will not give you the inheritance of my fathers." He lay on his bed sulking and refused to eat.

His wife Jezebel came in and asked him, "Why are you so sullen? Why won't you eat?" He answered her, "Because I said to Naboth the Jezreelite, 'Sell me your vineyard; or if you prefer, I will give you another vineyard in its place.' But he said, 'I will not give you my vineyard.' " Jezebel his wife said, "Is this how you act as king over Israel? Get up and eat! Cheer up. I'll get you the vineyard of Naboth the Jezreelite."

So she wrote letters in Ahab's name, placed his seal on them, and sent them to the elders and nobles who lived in Naboth's city with him. [1 Kings 21:1-8, NIV]

Did you catch the phrase at the conclusion of this passage? Verse 8 tells us that Jezebel "wrote letters in Ahab's name." We need to determine what this verse is saying to us. In other words, what does "in Ahab's name" mean?

Jezebel was writing to the elders and nobles as if she were King Ahab himself. Notice that she uses his seal; it was the seal that guaranteed to the receiver who the sender actually was. When the letters were received by the elders and nobles in Naboth's city, they would have believed that they had received correspondence from the king. In other words, Jezebel was writing on Ahab's behalf. The result was *as if* he had written the letters himself.

In our society today, we have a legal term for this—it's called a "power of attorney." A person who has "power of attorney" over another acts on the behalf of that other person. The transactions they make are the transactions the other would make if he or she were available to do so.

So! When we pray "in the name of Jesus," it's more than just tacking a few words on at the end of our prayer. It means praying *as if* we were praying in the place of Jesus. As far as prayer is concerned, we are His representative, we are His agent, we are His "power of attorney." It means that we are praying "according to His will."

As A Surrendered Believer

This is an awesome responsibility. It means I have to know what the will of God is. And that means I must be a serious student of the Word of God. Then I have to give up who I am, what I want, what I think, what I feel...

...and put on His wishes, His desires, His thoughts. It's all about Him, no longer about me.

It's all about submission—all about our full surrender unto God.

CHAPTER TEN

Limiting the Size of Your Barn

The question is easy, it's the answer that's so difficult. When we finally surrender our lives to God, we come face-to-face with this question: "How much is enough?" In other words, how big a house do I really need? How much is too much to spend on a car? What is a reasonable amount to spend on clothing and food and entertainment in a world where so many go to bed hungry every night without so much as a roof over their head?

These are serious questions every well-meaning Christian needs to ask himself and be prepared with an honest answer both for himself and God. Many people who call themselves Christian fail to come even close to encountering these matters on a personal level. Considering what we've learned so far about surrendering to God, what could possibly keep a person from examining his life and determining that what he has is more than it should be.

Undoubtedly, at least a small part of the explanation lies in what we call the American Dream. We've been taught from childhood that whatever we set our minds to, we can accomplish. If we desire wealth but were born to poverty, all we have to do is put our shoulder to the wheel and work our way into the kind of life the rest of the world merely dreams about. It's that old start-in-the-mailroom-and-work-your-way-to-the-top syndrome that possesses way too many of us in this country today. The borders of our nation are flooded with immigrants who want to buy into the American Dream. The universal goal of all mankind seems to be one of gaining control over one's own destiny and becoming something we currently are not.

The Parable of the Rich Man and His Barns

Jesus addressed the issue of our accumulating things in the parable that begins at Luke 12:16.

> **And he told them this parable: "The ground of a certain rich man produced a good crop. He thought to himself, 'What shall I do? I have no place to store my crops.' Then he said, 'This is what I'll do. I will tear down my barns and build bigger ones, and there I will store all my grain and my goods. And I'll say to myself, 'You have plenty of good things laid up for many years. Take life easy; eat, drink and be merry.'" '** [Luke 12:16-21]

What is our Lord describing for us here? Aren't we looking at the picture of a man who has accumulated so many riches for himself that he no longer has room to store them all? This is the American Dream turned American Dilemma. We have so many possessions that the walls of our gaudily-proportioned houses seem to be closing in around us and we need more places to stow our stuff.

Look at what the man in Jesus' story does when he runs out of space. Exactly the same thing the average American does when his space closes in on him—he builds bigger barns. Here in the United States of America, we are in the midst of a building explosion—not necessarily in the number of houses that are being built, but certainly in the size of these houses. Have you noticed? You may be old enough to remember the time when the two-bedroom house was considered spacious... it later became the three-bedroom house... and then the four. Today young couples are demanding five bedrooms and an office for the Mister, a playroom for the children, and even a scrap-booking room for the Mrs. One young family I know recently moved into a larger house. The husband was a little overwhelmed with the step they had just taken. "This house has five bathrooms," he exclaimed to me, "and there's only four in our family!" That's a long way from the one bedroom, one bath of yesteryear.

Why does something like this happen? We have only to look back at the three verses immediately preceding the telling of the parable of the rich man and his bigger barns that we read in Luke 12.

> **Someone in the crowd said to him, "Teacher, tell my brother to divide the inheritance with me." Jesus replied, "Man, who appointed me a judge or an arbiter between you?" Then he said to them, "Watch out! Be on your guard against *all kinds of greed*; a man's life does not consist in the abundance of his possessions."** [Luke 12:13-15 (NIV); italics added]

Immediately following these words, Jesus goes on to tell the parable of the rich man and his need to build bigger barns for all that he has accumulated. So in essence, how does Jesus label the rich man's behavior? Even before the telling of the story, he tags the rich man's accumulation as "greed."

He's saying that because of the man's greed, he accumulated so much stuff that he had to build bigger barns to accommodate his wealth. Most of us are reluctant to acknowledge the "greed" in our own backyard and we use all sorts of excuses to explain our desire for something bigger and better. The basic truth is—the cold hard fact according to Jesus' word is—it's greed that prompts us to accumulate more than we can store. Raw, unadulterated greed. Whether we admit it or not. That's what the Bible tells us. And we don't need a bigger house in which to store our "greed."

How does God view this propensity for greed in His people? How does the Father who gave us everything, including His only Son that we might have life... how does He view our obsessive attempts to accumulate more and more for ourselves and our family? We know the American Dream calls for our getting to the top, but how does God see us as we're making the climb? What's His perspective on our use of material wealth? Since all that matters in the long run is God's view on such issues, let's read in Luke chapter 12 to see what God has to say about the rich man's building bigger barns.

> **But God said to him, "You fool! This very night your life will be demanded from you. Then who will get what you have prepared for yourself?" This is how it will be with anyone who stores up things for himself but is not rich toward God. [Luke 12:20-21 (NIV)]**

Who is saying what to whom? It's all in that first sentence—God calls the rich man who's wrapped up in the accumulation of things... God calls him a fool. "Fool." Not something many of us would want to be called by God. Interesting, isn't it? The world would call such a person a success, yet God labels him as a fool.

I know, I know... some of you are claiming comfort in the wording of verse 21—telling yourself that the destiny God describes in this passage applies only to those who accumulate for themselves and are *not* rich toward God. You put the emphasis on the dual condition God lays out for us here. I won't belabor the point, but instead ask you to consider what Jesus tells us in Matthew 6:19-21 concerning our not storing up treasures on earth, but storing them up instead in heaven. Why would He say something like this? Because as He says, "where your treasure is, there your heart will be also." It's as simple as that.

So, when Luke 12:21 is read in light of the Matthew 6:19-21 passage, storing up treasure on earth *precludes* our being "rich toward God." Any way you slice it, "thing-accumulation" separates us from God. And that is not a condition the true believer would ever want to find himself in.

"Sell and Give to the Poor"

And not only that... if we return to our text in Luke 12 and read Jesus' teaching that follows the story of the rich man and bigger barns, we hear God pound the point home one more time.

> **And do not set your heart on what you will eat or drink; do not worry about it. For the pagan world runs after all such things and your Father knows that you need them. But seek his kingdom and these things will be given to you as well. Do not be afraid, little flock, for your Father has been pleased to give you the kingdom. *Sell your possessions and give to the poor...* [Luke 12:29-33a NIV (emphasis added)]**

All along, Jesus has been teaching that we must not accumulate treasures here on earth because these will steal our heart away from God. And now in this immediate passage, He's telling us to rid ourselves of such encumbrances if we've already collected them. You're probably thinking as I am thinking, "Surely He doesn't mean for us to take this literally today! What about the American dream?"

Ananias and Sapphira

I am reminded of the story of Ananias and Sapphira in Acts 5 and what Peter said in response to Ananias' claim that he'd sold his land and given the proceeds to the cause: "Didn't it [the land] belong to you before it was sold? And after it was sold, wasn't the money at *your* disposal?" (emphasis added) Implied in Peter's statement here is the fact that the selling of one's possessions was optional — Ananias could chose to sell or not to sell. If you read on, you will see Ananias' sin lay in his lying about what he had done in order to receive credit for something he had not done (i.e., he wanted his peers to *believe* that he had given it all rather than just a portion.) The point is God did not demand the selling of Ananias' possessions and the giving of all of it to the poor. Yet in the teaching to His disciples in Luke 12:29-33 (above), He orders them to do just that. Do we have a conflict here?

Because we know that all scripture is God-breathed (i.e., all of it comes out of the mouth of God according to 2 Timothy 3:16, and therefore all of it is truth), we know we must be able to resolve these two teachings that appear to be in conflict with the other. How do we go about doing that?

Everything Belongs to God

Look at it this way. It's possible that God is telling us that at all times He expects us to remember that He is the giver of all gifts. If our lives are fully surrendered to Him, then everything we have is His, including—but not limited to— all the material wealth that sometimes we believe we actually earned by ourselves. This would mean that whenever God asks us to give what we have to another, we have hearts that are willing to do just that. In the meantime, God allows us to enjoy for ourselves those gifts that He has given. The key lies in the condition of our hearts—whether or not we are willing to turn loose when He calls us to do so.

If we go about our daily routines with a heart that's bent on accumulating treasures in heaven rather than on earth... if at a moment's notice we are willing to give to others what He has given to us... then we should never have need to build bigger barns. That's a good thing. Based on the story Jesus tells about the rich man who used bigger barns as the solution to his accumulation problem, we know we can avoid playing the "fool" in God's eyes by keeping our lives on a simpler level. We must be careful, however, not to twist this teaching into a prohibition against owning earthly possessions. Jesus is not advocating a vow of poverty—just wanting us to turn loose of our innate desire to store up treasures here on earth.

Living in the land of plenty as we do, this is not an easy assignment. If you watch any TV at all, you are bombarded with reminders that what you have is not good enough—and you need to rush out and buy more. Your expensive Internet connection is not fast enough, your relatively new car is out of date, your computer obsolete, your jeans the wrong darkness and the list goes on and on. If we believe what the world tells us continually, it's hard to be satisfied with "less."

I own a perfectly good fifteen-year-old television set with a great picture. As little as I watch TV it should last me a good many more years before it breaks down and has to be replaced. But now the dimensions of the picture that's broadcast by the networks is changing and more and more of the programs have a black band across the top and bottom. I'm told that in a few years all programs will be like this and I will need a wide-screen plasma TV if I want to see a full picture without black bars. One salesman even told me I'd have to buy some sort of adaptor if I am going to receive a signal at all. It seems every day that it's harder and harder to be content with what I have.

How Much Is Enough?

How much is too much? No one can answer that question for you. It's something you have to work out for yourself, just between you and God. Based on what Jesus tells us in the scriptures we studied in this chapter, however, when you find yourself building bigger barns, you might possibly already be at that point of having too much.

For the surrendered believer, the answer to an over-accumulation problem lies not in bigger barns but in the godly use of the abundance that God has already given to you.

Raising the Barrier Against Materialism

- Make purchases based on product-usefulness rather than its status
- Be sure that it's an actual need you're satisfying and not just a want
- Reject everything that consumes your thoughts
- Develop a "give-it-away" habit
- Spend a day and remove everything that's not needed from a single room. Give these items to a charitable non-profit. REPEAT in every room of the house
- Say "yes" to every one of those phone calls soliciting donated items. Each time you fill a bag, go through your closets and your kitchen cupboards. If you give away only one bag in response to each call, over a period of time you will have cleared out a lot of unnecessary clutter
- Do not loan anything to friends or family—*give* it to them
- Enjoy things without having to own them
- Appreciate the beauties of nature—they are God's freebie to you
- Reject anything whose manufacture or sale promotes the oppression of other people
- Avoid "buy now, pay later" schemes
- If a possession or a project distracts you from seeking *first* the kingdom of God, get rid of it
- Remember that retirement is not your goal
- Determine that the Bible will be your standard and not the World

CHAPTER ELEVEN

Kissing the Hand of God

Perhaps the single-most identifiable characteristic distinguishing the surrendered believer from the nominal Christian is the degree to which Self is abandoned into the worship experience.

Self-abandonment is the natural posture of the surrendered believer. He has no concern that others might think him strange, nor does he have any need to impress those around him. Whether alone or in a corporate setting, his style may be reserved or lively or a little of both. The fact is, style simply doesn't matter. God created all of us to be different, and there are many different ways in which we can worship Him. No one way is necessarily better than another. In true worship there is an audience of only One. And that One is not looking for any specific body posture; He is looking for "heart."

Before we dig deeper into the subject of worship, we want to make sure we're all on the same page. When I use the word "worship" in the context of this chapter, there is no specific style of worship-service in mind; rather, we're looking at worship principles that apply across the board—whether it's a traditional, contemporary, gospel, or praise and worship setting. No matter the "order of worship," the involvement of the worshiper is always the same: the surrendered Christian participates, the non-surrendered or nominal Christian merely spectates.

If we were to boil the message of this chapter down to one key principle underlying the entire chapter, it would be this: "Worship is a full-body, contact sport." That is to say, it is *not* a spectator activity with people watching from the side-lines; it requires the full participation of the worshiper, and by "full" I mean everything the believer has and all that he is. As mentioned earlier, that participation may be reserved or lively or anywhere in between; but no matter what, the worshiper must play an active role in the worship activity, whether corporate or individual.

Defining the Word "Worship"

Think about a regular worship service at your church. In your mind, list the elements of a typical service that you would consider to be an act of worship. Whenever I give this assignment in a classroom setting, I hear responses like the singing, the sermon, prayer, the offering, the offertory. Sometimes I even get the response, "the announcements." People tend to list every element that shows up on "the order of worship" in their bulletin. I hope that by the time we complete this study, you will have a clearer idea of what constitutes worship, and what does not. You may even change your mind from where you are now, and that would not necessarily be a bad thing. It would just prove you know how to keep an open mind.

Let's look now at how "worship" is defined in scripture. The word itself is used in the Bible more than 180 times in addition to numerous, numerous examples of people worshiping God with their prayers and their service. The idea being conveyed is one of adoration, rendering homage to, serving, being pious towards, bowing down and falling prostrate before. These are all postures of worship.

By far the most commonly used Greek word in the New Testament that is translated "worship" is *proskuneo* (pronounced pros-koo-neh' –o.) This word stems from a root word meaning "to kiss as a dog licking his master's hand." It carries the idea of "fawning" or "crouching before." The picture is one of prostrating oneself in homage to another, adoring him, and paying reverence to him.

The word *proskuneo*, then, hints at something physical on the part of the worshiper. We said earlier that the surrendered believer may worship in a quiet, reserved manner or he may be more active and vocal in his approach—but either way there has to be actual participation. In the definition developed above, we're seeing that the involvement has to be one of attitude as well. This paves the way for quiet, meditative worship where the attitude of the heart is one of adoration and reverence. It also rules out more exuberant physical activity such as hand-raising and dancing if such activity is not accompanied with a heart focused entirely on the Lord. In other words, no matter the style of worship one chooses, the critical factor is the condition of the heart.

A Biblical Illustration of Worship

The first time the word "worship" is used in the Bible is in the story of Abraham's sacrifice of his son Isaac. First uses of a word give insight into the subtleties of its meaning. Let's return to the passage in Genesis 22 that we examined earlier in Chapter 3. That first time through we looked at the kind of trust the surrendered believer exhibits. In this chapter, we want to look at the same passage from the perspective of worship.

¹Some time later God tested Abraham. He said to him, "Abraham!" "Here I am," he replied.

²Then God said, "Take your son, your only son, Isaac, whom you love, and go to the region of Moriah. Sacrifice him there as a burnt offering on one of the mountains I will tell you about."

³Early the next morning Abraham got up and saddled his donkey. He took with him two of his servants and his son Isaac. When he had cut enough wood for the burnt offering, he set out for the place God had told him about. ⁴On the third day Abraham looked up and saw the place in the distance. ⁵He said to his servants, "Stay here with the donkey while I and the boy go over there. We will worship and then we will come back to you." |Genesis 22:1-5, NIV

Did you catch what Abraham said he and the boy were going to do? He said they would worship and return. Now this is the first time the word "worship" is used in scripture and it is used in connection with one of the greatest demonstrations of trust the world has ever seen. God told Abraham that he was to go to a place He would show him and that he was to sacrifice his son as a burnt offering there. Yet Abraham tells his servants that he and the boy will go to worship and *will return*. Obviously Abraham trusts God to spare his son in some way. He doesn't understand how, he just knows He will. So he complies with the instructions God gave him and prepares to sacrifice his son as a burnt offering—an event Abraham refers to in scripture as "worship."

What we want to zoom in on here is Isaac's role in all this. In verse 3 we learn that Abraham cut enough wood for the sacrifice and then in verse 6 (printed below) we learn that Isaac carries that entire quantity up the mountain side to the site on which the sacrifice would be made.

> **Abraham took the wood for the burnt offering and placed it on his son Isaac, and he himself carried the fire and the knife.**
> [Genesis 22:6a, NIV]

I don't know how much wood it takes to consume a human body, but I am quite sure it is more than a little boy can carry. Obviously, Isaac is old enough and consequently big enough to carry a load of sufficient size. This tells me he is also big enough to overpower his quite elderly father. Yet Isaac voluntarily chooses to enter into the worship experience with his father and allows himself to be bound upon the altar, knowing that his death is the ultimate end.

This says a lot. The first time we see the word "worship" in scripture it is associated with total commitment—total surrender—on the part of the worshiper. In other words, the surrendered believer gives everything that he is to the Lord when he worships. He holds back nothing for himself. This is full-contact worship at its best. And if you accomplish this sitting quietly in your pew, that's a good thing. If you need to stand and raise your hands heavenward or even fall prone before your Lord, that's equally good. Remember what we said earlier: God does not look at the things man looks at. Man looks at the outward appearance, but God looks at the heart. Our responsibility, then, is to be sure our heart is totally surrendered to Him.

The image of a bound Isaac lying on the altar reminds us of the instructions to the believers that we read in Romans 12:1-2. We've looked at that passage in Chapter 7, but now we want to look at just verse 1 and understand it in light of what we now know about worship.

> **Therefore, I urge you, brothers, in view of God's mercy, to offer your bodies as living sacrifices, holy and pleasing to God—this is your spiritual act of worship.** [Romans 12:1, NIV]

Just as Isaac was called to offer his body as a sacrifice to God in the Old Testament, we are being called to offer our bodies to Him in the New. Paul calls this offering our "spiritual act of worship." The New Testament teaching hasn't changed from the Old. God wants all that we are and nothing less will do. At one level, Isaac's situation differs from ours in that he faced physical death and God is asking for a living sacrifice in Romans 12:1. At another level, they're quite the same—both require dying to Self.

Additional Examples of Worship from Scripture

The Bible is filled with examples of worship. Let's look now at some illustrations found in the book of Revelation.

> **Who will not fear you, O Lord,**
> **and bring glory to your name?**
> **For you alone are holy.**
> **All nations will come**
> **and worship before you,**
> **for your righteous acts have been**
> **revealed.** [Revelation 15:4, NIV]

> **He said in a loud voice, "Fear God and give him glory, because the hour of his judgment has come. Worship him who made the heavens, the earth, the sea and the springs of water."** [Revelation 14:7, NIV]

There is an emotional response that is expressed in these two verses. Revelation 15:4 tells us that everyone fears God because God is holy (i.e., He is set apart, perfect and complete) and in Revelation 14:7 we fear Him because He is about to judge. Together we have the mandate to fear God because of Who He is (holy) and what He does (judges).

Way back In Chapter 2 we noted that the Bible commands us to fear God. In other words, the surrendered believer must not get so comfortable with God that she takes Him casually, but instead holds Him in proper esteem. He is God and we are not. We cannot comprehend the extent of His greatness and so we remain in awe of all He is and all He does; and in the context of worship, awe is analogous to reverential fear.

We may express this awe/fear in words or song; we may express it with silence. Again, style is not material. What matters in God's eyes is the attitude of our hearts.

Continuing on with additional examples of worship from the book of Revelation...

> **At this I [John] fell at his [the angel's] feet to worship him. But he said to me, "Do not do it! I am a fellow servant with you and with your brothers who hold to the testimony of Jesus. Worship God! For the testimony of Jesus is the spirit of prophecy."** [Revelation 19:10, NIV]

> **I, John, am the one who heard and saw these things. And when I had heard and**

seen them, I fell down to worship at the feet of the angel who had been showing them to me. [Revelation 22:8, NIV]

In these verses, we observe an example of one possible physical position for worship. John says that he falls at the feet of the angel in order to worship him. (Notice that in verse 10 the angel tells him not to do that, but to worship God instead.) Falling at the feet of another is a sign of surrender to that person. It's a picture of humbleness, submission, putting oneself in a vulnerable position. And that's the exact description of a relationship between the surrendered believer and the Father. This certainly makes it appropriate for us to fall prone before God at any time, but especially during our times of worship.

Sitting in the balcony during worship in a reserved congregation one Sunday, I observed a pastor on the first floor so overcome with reverence for his Lord that he fell to his knees—robes and all—and raised his hands high above his head. It would be easy for a man in his capacity to be concerned about how his parishioners might react to what they could perceive as undignified behavior. This pastor, however, chose to abandon Self fully to his worship. I doubt that he was even aware that others noticed him on the floor in front of his pew. I am quite certain that his worship was intended for that audience of One. That's what worship is all about.

The surrendered believer is comfortable on his knees before the Lord. Would that we all could do that more easily. Perhaps it is something we should be praying for on a regular basis during our quiet time alone with the Lord.

Before we leave the book of Revelation, let's take a look at the worship we might expect to see in heaven when we get there. The following passages take place in the throne room of God. In that holy and exalted realm, God sits center-stage and around Him are the four living creatures and twenty-four elders. For the purpose of this study, it isn't necessary that we understand the exact identity of these strange-sounding creatures; what we want to observe at this time is the nature of the worship that's going on in heaven.

> **Day and night they never stop saying: "Holy, holy, holy is the Lord God Almighty, who was, and is, and is to come." ⁹Whenever the living creatures give glory, honor and thanks to him who sits on the throne and who lives for ever and ever, ¹⁰the twenty-four elders fall down before him who sits on the throne, and worship him who lives for ever and ever. They lay their crowns before the throne and say: ¹¹ "You are worthy, our Lord and God, to receive glory and honor and power, for you created all things, and by your will they were created and have their being."** [Revelation 4:8c-11, NIV]

What strikes you most about this passage in Revelation 4? For me, it's the zealous praise, the beautiful words of devotion and adoration on the lips of the worshipers, but more than anything, it's the laying down of crowns at the feet of the Lord. This is a picture of one's giving up what is valuable to himself in order that the One he loves might enjoy it even more. This is selflessness at its best, a total abandonment of ones own needs and desires, and a complete focus on the object of one's worship.

This is what worship looks like in the surrendered believer. Isaac's willingness to lay on the altar shows us we must give up all that we are for Him; the twenty-four elders' laying down their crowns shows us that we give up all that we have.

> ⁸**And when he** [the Lamb that was slain] **had taken it** [the book that God held in His right hand], **the four living creatures and the twenty-four elders fell down before the Lamb. Each one had a harp and they were holding golden bowls full of incense, which are the prayers of the saints** ⁹**And they sang a new song:**
>
> **"You are worthy to take the scroll and to open its seals, because you were slain, and with your blood you purchased men for God from every tribe and language and people and nation.** ¹⁰**You have made them to be a kingdom and priests to serve our God, and they will reign on the earth."**
> [Revelation 5:8-10]

In this scene out of the fifth chapter of Revelation, we see the four living creatures and the twenty-four elders once again encircling the throne of their God in heaven. The Lamb has just taken the book with its seven seals from the hand of the One who sits on the throne. In appreciation of this monumental event, the elders and the living creatures once again fall down before the Lamb to worship Him. In the words that they sing, we hear the same devotion and adoration we heard in Revelation 4, but this time we also hear a great deal of thankfulness for all that Jesus the Lamb has accomplished. He gave His life in order to bring the men and women of this world to the Father so that they might serve Him as His priests here on earth.

Reading on in that same chapter in Revelation…

¹¹**Then I looked and heard the voice of many angels, numbering thousands upon thousands, and ten thousand times ten thousand. They encircled the throne and the living creatures and the elders.** ¹²**In a loud voice they sang:**
"Worthy is the Lamb, who was slain, to receive power and wealth and wisdom and strength and honor and glory and praise!"

¹³**Then I heard every creature in heaven and on earth and under the earth and on the sea, and all that is in them, singing: "To him who sits on the throne and to the Lamb be praise and honor and glory and power, for ever and ever!"**

¹⁴**The four living creatures said, "Amen," and the elders fell down and worshiped.**
[Revelation 5:11-14, NIV]

At this point, the volume is turned up in heaven. Myriads of angels—thousands upon thousands of them, ten thousand times ten thousand—surround the throne and lift blended voices to their Lord in praise. Just as we've seen before, the elders fall down at the feet of Him who sits on the throne. This is the way it goes every time—when worship is involved in Revelation 4 and Revelation 5, and again in Revelation 19 and 22, the worshiper falls down before the One he worships. How can the truly surrendered believer do anything less right here on earth? If anyone is willing to give all that he is, and all that he has in order to worship his Lord, then the only reasonable posture is one of humbleness, submission, and putting himself in a vulnerable position: on his knees or prone at the feet of God. This is our reasonable act of worship.

Worship as a Way of Life

The aim of this chapter is not to give a complete teaching on the subject of worship. We are looking at worship in this context only as it relates to giving control of our lives to God. So far we've seen that the act of true worship involves full surrender on the part of the believer. It stands to reason then that the surrendered believer *must* be involved in true worship. In Colossians 3:17 God tells us that in *everything* we do "whether in word or deed, [we are to] do it all in the name of the Lord Jesus, giving thanks to God the Father through him." If we apply this principle to the idea of worship, we see that worship is an on-going, continual activity in the life of the surrendered believer. This means that in addition to designated times of corporate and individual worship, the believer does everything he does in his work-a-day life as an act of worship.

Brother Lawrence was a monk who lived in France during the seventeenth century. His spiritual posture was simple: all day long he kept himself in the presence of God by continually conversing with Him. For Brother Lawrence, the set times for prayer and worship were no different from other times of the day. In the book, "The Practice of The Presence of God," Brother Lawrence writes: "I have ceased all forms of devotion and set prayers except those which my state requires. I make it my priority to persevere in His holy presence, wherein I maintain a simple attention and a fond regard for God, which I may call an actual presence of God." More simply put in modern-day English, Brother Lawrence walked in the presence of God, twenty-four-seven.

A number of years ago I came across another quote that is attributed to Brother Lawrence. It gives us a beautiful picture of worshiping God in everything that we do.

"I turn my little omelette [sic] in the pan for the love of God. When it is finished, if I have nothing to do, I prostrate myself on the ground and worship my God, who gave me this grace to make it, after which I arise happier than a king. When I can do nothing else, it is enough to have picked up a straw for the love of God. People look for ways of learning how to love God. They hope to attain it by I know not how many different practices. They take much trouble to abide in His presence by varied means. Is it not a shorter and more direct way to do everything for the love of God, to make use of all the tasks one's lot in life demands to show him that love, and to maintain his presence within by the communion of our heart with his? There is nothing complicated about it. One has only to turn to it honestly and simply."

"Doing everything for the love of God." What a perfect description of the surrendered believer! Taking captive every thought to make it obedient to Christ, doing everything that one does in life for Christ's sake rather than one's own, translating daily routine into worship experiences—these are the traits that separate the surrendered believer from the nominal Christian.

These are also the description of what great worship is all about.

Part III

The Joy of Full Surrender-Ship

CHAPTER TWELVE

Life as the Friend of God

Some things are so abrasive to your sense of right and wrong that you can never shake them out of your mind.

In a Sunday morning class that I was teaching as guest speaker, members of the class alternated presenting the opening prayer each Sunday. One particular Sunday, the young man who'd been designated for that morning's prayer stood and began in a loud, clear voice: "Hi, God! How're you doing today? I'm pretty good now, but I had a rough week. I'll bet you did too with all those people calling on you." To be honest, I didn't hear another word; my heart was still reeling from those opening lines.

What was so shocking about that morning's prayer? Palsy-walsy attitudes towards God, in my opinion, are offensive. And I believe this to be strongly substantiated in scripture. We'll be looking at some proof in just a little while.

In recent years there's been a movement afoot that encourages Christians to regard God as "friend." I do not take issue with the supposition, but I hasten to add that there is a right way and a wrong way to go about doing it. After all, God is God, and we are not. As such, He cannot be our pal, our buddy, our equal. To talk to Him as if He were on our level demonstrates a lack of understanding and an irreverence for who He is. According to the definition for blasphemy in Webster's 11th Collegiate Dictionary, an attitude of such familiarity would qualify as blasphemy.

We must not ignore the distance between God's lofty position and our lowly one.

Jesus Calls us "Friend"

The student of the Bible would jump right in at this point to remind me that Abraham was called the "friend of God" (2 Chronicles 20:7; Isaiah 41:8; James 2:23). Yes, and in addition to Abraham we have a number of other saints who had especially close relationships with God. The Bible tells us of people like Enoch who "walked with God"; Noah who "found favor in the eyes of the Lord"; Moses who spoke "face to face [with God] as a man speaks with his friend"; Job who refers to the time "when God's intimate friendship blessed [his] house"; and David whom God called "a man after my own heart" (Genesis 5:22, 6:8; Exodus 33:11; Job 29:4; Acts 13:22).

These were the Old Testament saints who had an intimate relationship with their Lord. In the New Testament, Jesus opens the door for all committed believers to take up that relationship as well.

> **I no longer call you servants, because a servant does not know his master's business. Instead, I have called you friends, for everything that I learned from my Father I have made known to you.** [John 15:15, NIV]

The context in which this particular verse resides is Jesus' conversation with His disciples shortly before His arrest, trial and execution. He is preparing them for His going away and their taking over the ministry. In this regard, He elevates their status from "servant" to full-fledged "friend." In the preceding verse (John 15:14), Jesus promises that if they obey His commands, they are His friends. Backing up one more verse to John 15:13, Jesus says that there is no greater love than laying down ones life for a friend. Knowing God, serving Him, obeying His commandments—the surrendered believer today certainly qualifies as one who can rightfully be called "the friend of God" just as the disciples of Jesus' day were called.

But Fear Is Still a Factor

From previous chapters, we know that the relationship of the surrendered believer to God is one of marked fear of Who God is, coupled with complete trust in everything He does. This fear would preclude any kind of buddy attitude in our relationship with God; yet total and complete trust opens the door to a true "friendship" along the lines of His relationship with Abraham, Moses, Enoch, Noah, Job and King David.

Reverence, fear—whichever you choose to call it—is the foundation on which our friendship with God is built. There is no "Hey, Pops!" about our relationship with Him; rather, it's a "Whatever you say, Father" attitude that we must exhibit. That is to say simply, our relationship is based on our giving Him the respect and honor and glory He demands and deserves.

Bottom Line

Friendship with God allows for a close, intimate relationship as a father to his child. Then, as a child to her father, the relationship is one of awe and total surrender unto His authority. This is not the relationship of one pal to another. After all, He is God and we are not.

CHAPTER THIRTEEN

God at the Center of Your Universe

At the point in one's life when total surrender is just about accomplished in full, Jesus becomes the epicenter of all life—ranking above family, career, and the distractions of every-day living. Choices are no longer predicated on one's personal desire, but on the will of God. Goals are more clearly defined. The believer has a better idea of who he is and he's quite comfortable with that image of himself. Life in general is less complicated and more rewarding. We now have a purpose and are equipped to know exactly what that purpose is. We feel close to God and converse with Him on a continual, on-going basis. He is our comforter, our motivator, our protector, our strength, our all in all.

These are just a few of the blessings that are ours once we surrender control of our lives to the Father, the Son and the Holy Spirit. With the accomplishment of that decision in our lives, we enter into an existence I refer to in this book as "out of control, and lovin' every minute of it!" I don't mean to imply that we don't have times after that point in which we slip up—as long as we're human, we *will* make mistakes—but rather that surrender to God has become the life-style and Self-in-control the exception.

As we transition from Self-centered to God-centered, we are more and more blessed. In the remaining chapters of the book, we'll explore a little of what living the surrendered life guarantees to the believer.

According to the Teachings of Paul

Read the works of the Apostle Paul and you quickly come to realize what it means to have God at the center of your universe. Paul persistently teaches that Christ is in us. In Colossians 3:4, he even refers to Christ as the One "who is our life"—which just about says it all. If Christ *is* our life, then everything revolves around Him; He's our all in all. In Galatians 2:20, we read:

> **I have been crucified with Christ and I no longer live, but Christ lives in me. The life I live in the body, I live by faith in the Son of God, who loved me and gave himself for me.** [Galatians 2:20, NIV]

Most of us are accustomed to the teaching that the Holy Spirit dwells in us (2 Tim 1:14; James 4:5), but here Paul tells us that Christ Himself also dwells in us. Then if you'll check out 1 John 4:12, you'll see that God lives in us as well. Bottom line: scripture is telling us that the Father, the Son and the Holy Spirit *all* indwell the surrendered believer. That's a power-house far bigger than anything we could ever imagine. So if the Father, Son and Spirit all reside in me, it would seem obvious that my life *must* be affected by their presence and that everything I do, say, think and feel will be centered around Them rather than Self.

And in Philippians 1:21, Paul puts it this way: "For to me, to live is Christ and to die is gain." It's an oft-repeated refrain of Paul's—pondering as to whether he would rather be with Jesus in heaven or doing Jesus' work right here on earth. Paul's conclusion? "To live is Christ," he says. In other words, living is for Christ; he prefers to stay. And we're back to Square One as stated in Colossians 3:4 above: Christ IS our life. In other words, when a person is surrendered to God, God is the center of his universe.

Finally, let's look at Colossians 3:1-3 and what it tells us about the triune God-head and the center of existence.

Since, then, you have been raised with Christ, set your hearts on things above, where Christ is seated at the right hand of God. Set your minds on things above, not on earthly things. For you died, and your life is now hidden with Christ in God.
[Colossians 3:1-3, NIV]

Whoa! That's a really, really strong command we're reading there. This statement makes it iron-clad that the life of the surrendered believer will be completely different from those around him. Did you catch it? Paul states it three different ways. As one who has been raised with Christ (i.e., "saved"), we are to: (1) set our hearts on the things above; (2) set our minds on things above; and (3) don't set our minds on earthly things.

That's a tall order for even the best of believers. According to Paul's teaching here, the surrendered believer no longer concerns himself with the demands of the work-a-day life. This doesn't imply that he doesn't do well at his job, take care of his family or enjoy the leisurely activities of life. He most definitely functions in the world as a responsible citizen, friend and family member, yet when it comes to setting priorities, even the smallest detail is based on what God/Jesus would want to happen rather than on what Self desires.

A Modern Day Example

Let me share a real-life example. I have a friend who does well in her line of business. She chooses to keep her life-style simple and use a great deal of the income God has blessed her with to further His kingdom in every way possible. When offered promotions, this woman prays long and hard before making any decision. It's not the additional income she concerns herself with; it's doing the will of God that's occupies her prayers. It's possible He wants her to accept the promotion so as to have even more income to devote to His work; or it may be that she should decline the offer in order to have the necessary time to continue the work He has set aside specifically for her to do.

There is no easy formula for us here. Each of us must spend time alone with God and listen to His directive for our life—on an individual basis. What's important to the surrendered believer is that we keep God at the center of our universe.

CHAPTER FOURTEEN

Freedom to Enjoy His Abundance

Just as knowing Jesus sets us free from the hold sin has on our lives, having God/Jesus at the center of our universe frees us to enjoy life to its fullest. In John 10:10 (NIV), Jesus tells us He came "that [we] might have life, and have it to the full." Another translation puts it this way: "...that [we] might have life and have it more abundantly." I think of this as living the "Abundant Life." It's what Jesus gives us when we turn control of our lives over to Him.

There is no shortage of scriptural references that give us the picture of what this abundant life is all about. I've printed out a limited selection of these for you below:

> **His divine power has given us everything we need for life and godliness through our knowledge of him who called us by his own glory and goodness. [2 Peter 1:3, NIV]**

> **"And why do you worry about clothes? See how the lilies of the field grow. They do not labor or spin. Yet I tell you that not even**

Solomon in all his splendor was dressed like one of these. If that is how God clothes the grass of the field, which is here today and tomorrow is thrown into the fire, will he not much more clothe you, O you of little faith? So do not worry, saying, 'What shall we eat?' or 'What shall we drink?' or 'What shall we wear?' For the pagans run after all these things, and your heavenly Father knows that you need them. But seek first his kingdom and his righteousness, and all these things will be given to you as well." [Matthew 6:28-33, NIV]

Every good and perfect gift is from above, coming down from the Father of the heavenly lights, who does not change like shifting shadows. [James 1:17, NIV]

And we know that in all things God works for the good of those who love him, who have been called according to his purpose. [Romans 8:28, NIV]

...and you have been given fullness in Christ, who is the head over every power and authority. [Colossians 2:10, NIV]

These are just a sampling of the riches God promises the surrendered believer. In these verses, we see that we have everything we need—all the good and perfect gifts raining down upon us from above. It seems there's just about nothing God won't do for those who are committed to serving His kingdom. He even takes the obstacles that deter our work and turns them around so that they work for good rather than evil.

We need never fear incompetence; He makes us whole and complete so that we are up to whatever task He calls us to do. What we lack in ourselves is made full in Christ; in other words, we are made whole and complete by our association with Christ Jesus alone.

From these selected verses, it's easy to see that sense of security and competence the believer enjoys whenever she fully surrenders her life to God. But just in case we miss the point, God spells it out for us one more time in Romans 8.

Therefore, there is now no condemnation for those who are in Christ Jesus, because through Christ Jesus the law of the Spirit of life set me free from the law of sin and death. [Romans 8:1-2, NIV]

Now that's security if ever there was any. Once we put Jesus at the helm, we are no longer living in any sort of condemnation. Oh we must confess and repent whenever we sin (and believers do sin, I'll say it again), but we are assured of forgiveness so as never to have to live with the guilt of our sin again.

After I accepted Jesus Christ as Lord and Savior but before I had turned control of my life over to Him, I was riddled with guilt. The time of greatest attack was most often as I stood before the mirror to curl and fix my hair every morning before leaving for work. I am convinced God has a sense of humor because in those days my hair took a full hour of fussing before it was ready to go. That hour was a time of great torment for me! Try as I would, there was no pushing out of my mind the thoughts of the bad things I'd done to those I loved. But as I learned to surrender all of me to God, that sense of guilt faded and I was able to enjoy the blessings of the Abundant Life.

Within the scope of this book we cannot possibly cover the full extent of the Abundant Life, but let's pick up one last reference before moving on. It's from Galatians Chapter 5—you're probably very familiar with it.

> **But the fruit of the Spirit is love, joy, peace, patience, kindness, goodness, faithfulness, gentleness and self-control. Against such things there is no law.** [Galatians 5:22-23, NIV]

Just bask a moment in the truth of what you're reading here—these are the "fruit" that is yours once you surrender your life to Jesus. I don't want you to slide over the full impact of what God is saying here. He's saying that if we have the Holy Spirit (and we do if we have Jesus) then we have each of the qualities listed above: love, joy, peace, patience, kindness, goodness, faithfulness, gentleness and self-control. "But I don't *feel* like I have patience," you say. But you *do*—that's what scripture is telling us here. If you don't *feel* like it, and if you don't see it operating in your life, then you simply have to reach way-down deep inside and bring it up into play. The same is true with any of the virtues that accompany the indwelling of the Spirit. Each element of the "fruit of the Spirit" is there from the inception of our rebirth. Our responsibility is to bring each to light so that it affects the way we live.

Jesus promised it; so it has to be true: The surrendered believer has everything he needs to live out the Abundant Life.

CHAPTER FIFTEEN

Contentment in Weakness

W e're looking at the joy that comes our way once we have relinquished control of our lives to the One who controls all existence. In the previous section we saw that there are certain material and spiritual blessings that come to the one who surrenders his or her life to the Lord. The Apostle Paul was one of the most surrendered persons known to mankind throughout all history. He suffered a great deal in his service to God, but he was also immensely blessed. Through him, God brought about many miracles. This brought Paul a great deal of fame and notoriety among the people of his day. But through it all, Paul continually insisted that if there is any boasting to be done, it was to be done solely about God and His power, not Paul's own. Listen to a part of Paul's explanation in the twelfth chapter of his second letter to the church in Corinth.

> **[7]To keep me from becoming conceited because of these surpassingly great revelations, there was given me a thorn in my flesh, a messenger of Satan, to torment me. [8] Three times I pleaded with the Lord to take it away from me. [9]But he said to**

me, "My grace is sufficient for you, for
my power is made perfect in weakness."
Therefore I will boast all the more gladly
about my weaknesses, so that Christ's
power may rest on me. ¹⁰That is why, for
Christ's sake, I delight in weaknesses, in
insults, in hardships, in persecutions, in
difficulties. For when I am weak, then I am
strong. [2 Corinthians 12:7-10, NIV]

There are several teaching points that we could pull from
this passage, but we need to stick with the topic at hand. Paul
is telling us about God's response to his repeated request to
have the "thorn" taken from his flesh. God's answer is significant. "My grace is sufficient for you," He says, "for my
power is made perfect in weakness." God's power is made
pure, total, complete, lacking-in-nothing just because Paul
has a weakness in his body, mind or spirit—we are not told
which. It's through Paul's shortcomings that God shines; and
it's through our shortcomings that He does as well.

In 1 Corinthians 1:27 [NIV] we learn that God chooses
"...the weak things of the world to shame the strong." In
other words, we were chosen *because of* our weaknesses!
And how does that "shame the strong"? Because whenever the surrendered believer exhibits a weakness or flaw
of any kind, God steps in with His power and takes over.
Witnesses have the opportunity, then, to see God at work in
that individual.

This is an important precept to me. When I was growing
up, I had a very loud voice. Aunts and uncles, grandparents
and parents alike were continually telling me to be quiet—
sometimes in not very kind tones. Try as I would, I didn't
seem to have much control over the volume. Whenever I
was agitated, the voice shouted, someone complained and
I shrank away in shame. I learned to hate the sound of my

own voice and over time became a little reticent in my dealings with others; it just wasn't worth the pain. As an adult, after I had surrendered my life to Jesus, a wonderful thing happened. The voice didn't change, but the reactions of those listening to me did.

I remember the first time I noticed it—an elderly woman came up to me after a prayer circle ended in a small-town church in Texas. She wanted to thank me for leading the prayer for the group that morning. In her words, "It was the first time I was able to hear what was being said." My loud voice was now a blessing? Not much later I was called to speak before a good-sized group in the sanctuary of a church I was visiting. The sound system was not working that Sunday morning and I discovered I could project to the corners of the room easily and without amplification. Over the years, my ability to project has become a real asset in the fight against Satan, who loves to attack sound systems in the churches where believers are on the march.

God took a weakness in me—the inability to control the volume of my speech—and he turned it into a blessing both for me and for others. I may not know what Paul's weakness was, but I am certainly aware of the work God accomplished through him using that weakness. This is what He does for every believer who surrenders his or her weakness to Him.

There are times still when my lack of control over the volume of my voice gets me into hot water—especially on the home front—but all in all, I am quite content that God is using this particular weakness for good. When we fully surrender to Him, we are freed from worry and concern about the chinks in our armor. Our little imperfections become God's arena of brilliance. We have His assurance that He will step up to bat and take up the slack.

143

CHAPTER SIXTEEN

Knowing the Purpose
of Your Life

It's really easy in life to become successful at what you are doing and still have an emptiness so big there's nothing you can do to satisfy it. For years I chased the almighty dollar and ended up making good money; but that wasn't nearly enough. I wanted the best and was willing to sacrifice whatever it took to get myself there. Whether it was working well into the night, giving up weekends, or problem-solving while trying to sleep, I was willing to do whatever was needed. But the "top" managed always to stay a few inches beyond reach. No matter how high I went, there was always more power, more authority, more influence to be acquired than what I currently had.

One of the great joys of surrendering to Christ is that, in the process, we learn the specific purpose God has for us as individuals. The beauty of that is, when we are operating within the realm of God's calling on our life, the driving forces that torment us and keep satisfaction at bay are finally satisfied. We are content within our successes. And we are content with our weaknesses. Listen to Paul's commentary on contentment:

¹¹I am not saying this because I am in need, for I have learned to be content whatever the circumstances. ¹²I know what it is to be in need, and I know what it is to have plenty. I have learned the secret of being content in any and every situation, whether well fed or hungry, whether living in plenty or in want. [Philippians 4:11-12, NIV]

This was a real eye-opener for me. Before Christ, I was hell-bent on finding satisfaction in my career. In the verses above, Paul says he learned how to be content during bad times as well as in good. And that's the secret. True contentment has nothing to do with material success or the physical realm in any way. True contentment is found in our pursuing the assignment God has ordained for us individually. That means true contentment is reserved for those who have surrendered their will to His and are walking in the realm of His calling on their life.

I knew within a few short days following my surrender to Christ that God was calling me to teach. As far as the when, where and how, the call was non-specific, but it was very clear to me that I was not being called into the clergy or to be a Bible scholar; but to study as a lay person and to turn right around and teach others what God was teaching me. My calling was to study *and teach*, not just study. But for the first two years no teaching assignment was forthcoming. For the time being, I was content with the six hours of study I was giving it each day. But by the end of two years I was beginning to wonder if I had misunderstood the call.

Then at the beginning of the third year, opportunity came. Slowly at first, then escalating to the point where I was teaching four classes a week. The point I'm making here is that contentment didn't hold off until I was finally "successful" as a Bible teacher; it was there from the time I first sat down at my desk to begin my six hours a day. Why? Because it was at that time that I first began operating within the sphere of the gifts God had given me and the calling He had placed on my life.

We are happiest and most content when we are doing exactly what God wants us to be doing.

How Can I Know God's Purpose for My Life?

In Jeremiah 29:11, God says "I know the plans I have for you, plans to prosper you and not to harm you, plans to give you hope and a future." And in Ephesians 2:10, He tells us we are "...[His] workmanship, created in Christ Jesus to do good works, which [He] God prepared in advance for us to do."

Long before we were formed in our mother's womb, God knew the specific task He would assign to each of us. And if God wants us to carry out that assignment during our lifetime, then He's going to have to make it known to us. And that He does. Our responsibility is simply to listen as He lays out His plan before us.

You can find many books on the shelves of your local Christian bookstore that outline methods and inventories and the like that are designed to help you determine what God has called you to do. These can be helpful and many have used them to find their place of service for the Lord. I believe, however, there's a cheaper and much simpler way; and here's the "1, 2, 3" of it: (1) Make a list of the things you like to do. (2) Determine what kind of things you do the best. And (3) ask your spouse, friends, mentors and clergy persons in what activities they see the most "fruit" in your life. Chances are there will be a common activity or two running through lists "1, 2, and 3." This is your area of service.

The rationale behind this simple system is in itself very simple. God gives us talents and abilities and He expects us to use them for His glory. Because they are from God, we are going to be good at activities that use these gifts. And when we're good at something, we tend to enjoy doing it. Being good at it and enjoying it produces results that others are able to see. There you have it: God calls, He equips, and He arranges for us to see the fruit of our labors.

I had a dear friend once who was called upon to nurse his step-father and then later his mother through the final illnesses in each of their lives. Caring for the sick was something he'd never done and certainly wasn't anything he'd ever imagined he would enjoy. Strictly out of duty to his aging parents, my friend—we'll call him Roger—began making weekly trips to the plains of western Oklahoma to spend a few days feeding, dressing, bathing and otherwise caring for his parents before returning back home to his wife and family. As the weeks turned into months, and he continued to drive the several hundred miles to his patients' bedside on a regular basis, Roger was surprised to find that he actually enjoyed his new role as nurse-maid. He found it peaceful and rewarding. But even more astonishing to him was the fact that, no matter how demanding the schedule became towards the end, he never tired physically of taking care of his parents. In fact, he would tell me later, the more dependent they became on him and the more physical exertion that was required as the end neared, the more God strengthened him and empowered him so that he was always up to the task. God even kept him wide-awake for the long drive home—exhausted and late at night.

Roger was operating in the sphere of God's calling on his life; he had discovered his gift of mercy.

That's just the way it works. Try it out. Jump into action right now doing something for God—anything—and let Him direct your path to The Assignment that He created specifically for you. He'll get you there... because He wants you to accomplish His will in your life.

There's an old story out of Africa that sums up the point we're trying to see here.

> **Every day in Africa, a gazelle wakes up. He knows that he must run faster than the fastest lion or he will be killed. Every day in Africa, a lion wakes up. He knows that he must run faster than the slowest gazelle or he will starve to death. So it makes no difference whether you are a lion or a gazelle; when you wake up in the morning, you'd better be running.**

This isn't to say that the Lord helps him who helps himself. What it's saying is we have to do our part according to the instructions He has given us. Just as Jesus directed the blind man to go wash the spittle from his eyes in the pool of Bethsaida, He's asking us to get involved and step out in faith. When the blind man complied with the instruction, Jesus restored his sight. When we comply, God opens our eyes for us to see for ourselves The Assignment He has given us to do.

Once again, it all boils down to our willingness to surrender to Him—totally and completely. As we turn control over to God, He accomplishes His purpose in our lives and we are blessed as a result of it.

CHAPTER SEVENTEEN

Hearing God When He Speaks

Have you ever heard yourself saying, "If only God would tell me what He wants me to do." Your heart wants to do nothing except what Jesus wants you to do. You've even figured out in what arena He is directing you to serve, and that's where you're operating. But when it gets down to the details of how to bring about The Assignment, you have no idea what He would have you to do next. You pray for enlightenment, but you still haven't heard how to proceed.

The heart that is surrendered to God is equipped with a new sensitivity that enables it to hear the small, quiet nudgings from God. I call this extra sensory ability, "listening with the ears of our heart." Here it is in action:

> "Robert" was visiting a patient in the hospital. After his visit was completed, he stopped by to see his sister who worked at the same hospital. In the middle of their conversation, Robert suddenly got up and excused himself. The sister followed suit and walked with him to the hospital entrance where they said their good-byes.

As she left her brother at the door and turned to go back to her office, the sister heard Robert ask someone if he needed help. She didn't know what happened next until later when Robert called to explain.

His abrupt departure had been prompted, Robert told her, by a sudden nudging that he needed to leave the hospital immediately. Without questioning, he got up from his chair and headed for the car. As Robert entered the parking lot, he saw a man struggling to hoist his wheel chair into the trunk. He appeared to be making little headway so Robert asked if he could help. He sent the man on to wait in the car while he (Robert) packed the wheel chair away in the trunk. Then he went to the window and asked if there was anything else he could do to help.

The man told him "yes," he needed prayer. He'd just left ICU where the doctors had taken his wife off the ventilator. He needed comfort. There in the middle of the hospital parking lot, Robert took the man's hand and began to pray. Afterward, the man smiled at Robert and called him a "godsend."

It's truly amazing, isn't it, that God puts us exactly where He needs us in order to go to work for Him. We must be attentive so as to hear God when He calls. Had Robert not heeded the nudging when he did, he surely would have missed the man in desperate need of prayer. But because Robert knows how to "listen with the ears of his heart," he was available when God called and he was used for God's glory.

An interesting side note here—both Robert and the man he ministered to are pastors of churches in the same town. God had found a way to have one man of God minister unto another.

Robert long-ago surrendered control to the One who controls the universe. And because his heart is surrendered to God, he hears with his heart the nudgings of God's voice. Every surrendered believer has the ability to hear God in this same way. The more continually we find ourselves in that state of "out of control," the more consistently we are able to hear the Master's voice.

A believer who is fully surrendered can expect to hear from God on a continual basis. That's one of the great blessings of giving your life to Jesus.

CHAPTER EIGHTEEN

A Simplified Life

Once we have successfully surrendered to God, it's not surprising to realize that life has just become a whole lot simpler.

A friend of mine says that she's a "fixer" by nature. All her life, she has enjoyed fixing things around her. She likes to take old furniture and "fix it up" so it's like new again. When her children were young, she mended their broken toys. If the toaster doesn't pop, she takes it apart. If a drawer is stuck or anything else needs fixing, she's right on top of it. This is what she enjoys doing with her time. And I say, "What a great person to have around the house!"

Yet the person who is continually fixing their own problems can find it difficult to turn anything over to God. He or she tends to turn to Self first and God as a last resort.

Imagine how much simpler life would be without the cares and worries of everyday life weighing us down. God tells us in 1 Peter 5:7 that we are to give all our cares and worries to Him because He cares about what happens to us. The surrendered believer is able to live this out in his life, because he has surrendered control of everything to God. He knows that the first line of defense against any problem is "taking it to God in prayer." Before discussing it with a friend, before running to the doctor, *before* trying to fix anything on his own, he falls to his knees and he talks with God.

And he leaves it there.

Maybe it's time to take inventory of what's going on in your life today. Take a blank sheet of paper and list the things you hang onto on a daily basis. Your list might include things like being concerned about having enough money to pay the bills this month, finding the time to fix supper before Cindy's soccer game and still get Luke to baseball practice on time; or maybe you have ailing parents in Topeka who need you at their bedside but you have a spouse and young children at home in Tulsa who need your attention as well.

It really doesn't matter whether we're rich or poor, old or young, male or female. When it comes to life's everyday problems, we're all pretty much the same. If we cling to our troubles and try to fix them ourselves, eventually we break. It's so unnecessary. God invites us to surrender all our concerns to Him and then to trust Him for the outcome. In Chapter 3 of this book, we saw how Shadrach, Meshach, and Abednego knew all about this. "Our God will save us," they said when faced with the possibility of a fiery death if they did not forsake God, "but even if He doesn't..." They had turned the problem over to God and the outcome was no longer in their hands. Life for them had just become a whole lot simpler.

The same is true for every surrendered believer. We have only to take God up on His offer and turn all our cares and worries over to Him. It sounds simplistic; but if we can refrain from pulling our troubles back, it's guaranteed to work.

CHAPTER 19

Freedom From Addictive Behavior

I do not intend this chapter to be a comprehensive discourse on the subject of addiction. We'll leave that to the experts on substance abuse. What I'm talking about here is anything that occupies our thoughts to the point that it distracts from God. Such activities might include "the bigs," but are certainly not limited to them.

Before we move on, take a moment to think about what you think about most. Write it down so that you can see what it is you're committed to. Maybe it's shopping, maybe it's watching golf on TV, or working out at the gym. Or maybe you're in the process of redecorating the house, and you're working out the different color-schemes in your head. Perhaps you're worried about world situations, or a child who's struggling with a learning disability. The possibilities are limitless.

In themselves, none of these things are bad, but each has the potential for separating us from God. That's bad.

I had a neighbor once who obsessed on running. This was during a time when jogging was very much in and everyone was trying to get outside and do a little of it. In other words, it was the "normal" thing to do. On any given Saturday morning, however, I'd watch my neighbor-lady leave the neighborhood on foot, bright and early; then later in the day I would cross her path again as I was out and about running errands around town, sometimes a great distance from the house. Once I came across her running in three different parts of town and covering a time span from daybreak to dusk. As the seasons progressed into years, this woman became leaner and leaner until she looked like a skeletal frame stretched-over with skin that had weathered to a deep black-brown. Both the progressive weight-loss and the unnatural-looking tan pointed to addiction. It was as if she just couldn't get enough. The more she ran, the greater her need for running just a little bit more. I'm this way with carbohydrates; some of you may relate. Eat a few too many and my cravings increase exponentially; be reasonable about my intake and I do okay. The same is true with just about anything. Moderation and balance are the key.

Besides the obvious damage such "addictions" inflict on our bodies and minds, consider what happens to our relationship with God. With thoughts that are consumed with the subject of our addiction, there's little room left for God and we drift away. Pretty soon, our backs are turned completely to Him and we're facing directly into the antithesis of God. Every step from that point on takes us farther and farther from the triune God-head.

Fortunately, the solution to all this is simple: immersion in prayer and the study of God's Word keeps our thoughts focused on Him and He at the center of our universe. We said it in Chapter 12, but it bears repeating here: this in no way implies that we are to be so immersed in God that we are dysfunctional in the world in which He placed us. Quite the contrary. The surrendered believer continues to operate as responsible citizen, loyal friend and loving family member *as* he keeps his heart connected to God in everything that he says, does and feels.

Scripture tells us that we become like that which we worship. If our life is primarily focused on the things of the world (that feed our addictions) then our obsession with such things is intensified. If on the other hand our life is focused around God, His purpose and His plan, then we become more godly and the things of the world fade by comparison.

It's a matter of priorities; and the surrendered believer puts God before all things.

CONCLUSION:

A Final Look at Grace

If at this point you're thinking things look a little hopeless and that you're so far off God's standard it'll never work for you, take heart—you are not alone. We are all human and quite frankly we all fall way off the mark. But God is God and He knows the desires of our heart. He doesn't just look at what we are doing in the here and now, but also at the attitude of our hearts and what He knows we will become in due time. We have only to look at some of the heroes of scripture to see that God's "saints" were really no more perfect than we.

Let's look at Father Abraham as an example. Abraham was so special that God selected Him from among all the peoples of the earth to be the progenitor of the people He would call His own. In other words, it would be from Abraham's seed that the chosen people of God would descend, as would also eventually the Savior of this world—the Messiah, the Lord Jesus Christ. (Incidentally, it's important to note here that God later confirmed this covenant with Abraham's son Isaac, not Ishmael; and after that, with Isaac's son Jacob, and not Esau. There can be no doubt then that God's people descend from the twelve tribes of Jacob and that all the land and other promises God made in Genesis belong to the descendents of Abraham *through* Jacob's twelve sons and none other.)

Scripture does not tell us that God selected Abraham because Abraham was perfect. In fact, we are given the picture of a man who was far from perfect. In Genesis Chapter 12, shortly after his calling from God, Abraham takes his wife to Egypt and tells her she must lie to the Egyptians and tell them that she is his sister so that no one will kill him in order to get to her. Then in Genesis Chapter 20, he lies to Abimelech king of Gerar about Sarah's being his sister so that Abimelech will not kill him. Here's a man who put his own safety above protecting the sexual integrity of his wife—twice—and yet God selects him to father a nation from which the Christ would descend. In the book of Romans, the apostle Paul refers to Abraham's faith as being "credited to him"—added to Abraham's side of the ledger through no effort on Abraham's part. And remember, that's exactly what Ephesians 2:8-9 tells us: that our salvation has nothing to do with our own efforts; it is entirely a gift from God.

In other words, God simply called Abraham righteous and it became so regardless of the unrighteous acts in his life. Why did God do this? In both Galatians 3:6 and James 2:23, the scriptures tell us that Abraham "believed God" and then it was credited to him as righteousness. It was the attitude of his heart that mattered most to God. Abraham wasn't perfect, but God gave him credit for being so.

Look at David. God called David a "man after His own heart." Yet David lusted after a married woman, seduced her, and when she became pregnant with his child, David arranged for the murder of her husband. No way any of us would call that righteous behavior; yet God forgave David when he confessed, repented, and turned his life around. In other words, David wasn't perfect, but God gave him credit for being so.

There are also stories about kings of Judah during the days of the divided kingdom that show us God does not expect perfection in man in the short-run. Kings Asa,

Jehoshaphat, Joash, and Hezekiah had their weak moments, yet God said of each one of them: "He did what was right in the eyes of the Lord." In other words, God's over-all evaluation of them—in spite of their humanity—was that they were righteous. They were not perfect, but God gave them credit for being so.

The point here is God's "saints" are not perfect, but God gives us credit for being so. That raises the question then: Does this mean we can do anything we want and not worry at all about reaching God's standards? Of course not. That's been the point of this entire book—the true believer is defined by his adherence to the standards the Bible sets for belief and behavior. If we are called to perfection and yet as human beings we're not capable of perfection, what is the answer? Peter deals with this in his first letter.

[1]Therefore, rid yourselves of all malice and all deceit, hypocrisy, envy, and slander of every kind. [2]Like newborn babies, crave pure spiritual milk, so that by it you may grow up in your salvation, [3]now that you have tasted that the Lord is good.

[4]As you come to him, the living Stone— rejected by men but chosen by God and precious to him— [5]you also, like living stones, are being built into a spiritual house to be a holy priesthood, offering spiritual sacrifices acceptable to God through Jesus Christ. [1 Peter 2:1-5, NIV]

Two phrases I want to draw to your attention: "grow up in your salvation" (v.2) and "being built into a spiritual house to be a holy priesthood" (v.5). These phrases clearly imply an on-going process as opposed to a finite point in history.

163

What could it possibly mean to "grow up" in our salvation other than to become more and more deserving of what God has already given us. As we mature in our faith, we become more and more like Jesus and therefore more and more righteous. The passage also tells us that we are "being built"— transformed from what we are now to the holy priesthood that we eventually will be when we stand before our Lord in the throne room of heaven.

Read the passages below and notice how Paul adds to Peter's teaching that perfection is a process rather than a one-time event.

> **¹⁰And we pray this in order that you may live a life worthy of the Lord and may please him in every way: bearing fruit in every good work, growing in the knowledge of God, ¹¹being strengthened with all power according to his glorious might so that you may have great endurance and patience, and joyfully ¹²giving thanks to the Father, who has qualified you to share in the inheritance of the saints in the kingdom of light.** [Colossians 1:10-12, NIV]

> **We ought always to thank God for you, brothers, and rightly so, because your faith is growing more and more, and the love every one of you has for each other is increasing.** [2 Thessalonians 1:3, NIV]

Paul agrees that there is a growing process the surrendered believer progresses through. After accepting Jesus Christ as Lord and Savior, we continue to grow until one day in heaven we stand before Jesus and we are like Him— perfect in every way.

Well, there you have it. The bottom line is simple: the Word of God lays out for us the high standard God has set for His people. God is good; He does not demand such standards over-night. Instead, He looks at the heart to determine its motives and weighs our behavior in light of how much we have grown.

One fact is certain. If you have truly surrendered your life to the Lord Jesus Christ, there will be evidence of that surrender in the way you live out your life. The work of grace that God began in you will succeed in shining through.

That's our hope. And it's God's promise.

Printed in the United States
64356LVS00001B/1-177